MW00474802

Exposed Heart

Exposed Heart

Jackie Holland

Bridge-Logos *Publishers*

Gainesville, Florida 32614 USA

Exposed Heart
by Jackie Holland
Copyright © 2000 by Bridge-Logos Publishers
Library of Congress Catalog Card Number: pending
International Standard Book Number: 0-88270-827-9

Published by:
Bridge-Logos *Publishers*
PO Box 141630
Gainesville, FL 32614
http://www.bridgelogos.com

Contents

Chapter One

Nobody's Fool

My hands trembled as I aimed my .25 caliber pistol at my husband, who stood only a few feet away from me. If he took one more step toward the door I knew I would pull the trigger. I was sick and tired of playing the part of a fool who looked the other way as he flaunted his adulterous relationship and gambling addiction. After three failed marriages, I wasn't about to let this man, or any other man, abuse me and think he could just walk out the door! This time I was going to have the last word.

I've often wondered how my life could have taken such a destructive turn. I was reared in a loving Christian home by my parents, Elaine and Woodrow Jackson. I never questioned my parents' love for the Lord or for each other. Theirs was a time-tested relationship, weathered by years of pain and hardship.

It seemed that no matter how early I got up or how late I went to bed, my father was seated in his favorite chair reading his well-worn Bible by the light of a small lamp. His passion for God and the Bible was as genuine as the golden sunset stretching over the Texas horizon. His love for his family was just as beautiful.

My mother's dedication to the Lord was equally apparent. She saw to it that we were in church every time the doors were open. Sunday morning, Sunday night, Wednesday night, and at every revival service in between, she made sure our family was sitting in church wearing our best outfits. She starched and pressed our clothes until they were so stiff, I do believe they could have sat in church without us in them!

Things hadn't always been this way in the Jackson household. Until the year I was born, my father had a severe drinking problem. His parents weren't churchgoing people. Who's to say whether or not they were Christians? His upbringing may explain his reluctance to go to church during the early years of his marriage to my mother.

My mother, however, was brought up in a home where the love of Jesus was taught and practiced. But that didn't shield her from tragedy. At a very young age, in fact, she witnessed the brutal murder of her father.

Her father had been called as a witness to testify against an alleged killer. Just days before the trial was scheduled to begin, a stranger rode up to their house and called for her father to come outside.

This was back in the days when men supposedly settled things like men. Justice could just as easily be enforced by a bullet in the gut as by a judge in a courtroom. Unfortunately, justice wasn't served either way when this stranger shot the man who would be my grandfather—right in front of his wife and children. He bled to death as they stood by, shocked and helpless.

My grandmother, whom we affectionately and appropriately called "Big Mama," never dated anyone after my grandfather was killed. She spent the rest of her days working hard to care for her fatherless children.

The remaining years of my mother's childhood were sad ones. She wanted a father, and rightly so. At fifteen, she married my father, and soon they began a family. As a farmer, my father worked long and hard hours to provide for his growing family, but on the weekends he drank. They say he could never stop with just one drink. He'd drink until he was drunk, sometimes passing out in a ditch. My mother kept praying and believing that God would save him and deliver him from his addiction to alcohol.

One night, when my mother least expected it, her prayers were answered. It happened during a midweek revival service. It wasn't unusual for my father to go to church. However, he would stay outside during the entire service, talking shop with several of his buddies until church was over. When he did actually attend a service or revival meeting, often it was to appease my mother after his usual weekend drinking bouts.

This night something was different. God dealt with my father at the core of his being, and his life changed forever. Somehow the Holy Spirit had broken through to his hardened heart as the invitation to receive Christ as Savior was extended. My father says his body began trembling from his head to his toes. His legs shook so much that he had to lean on my mother for support as the two made their way to the front of the small country church. The Holy Spirit had gripped his soul, and suddenly, heaven and hell were realities he couldn't afford to ignore.

The day he asked Jesus to be his Lord and Savior was the day my father quit drinking. Period. From that day on, he never touched another drop of liquor—and he began telling everyone who would listen about Jesus. There's no doubt in my mind that the faith-filled prayers my mother prayed over the years set each member of our family on the road to salvation. Acts 16:31 affirms this: "Believe in the Lord Jesus Christ, and you will be saved—you and your household." I will be forever thankful to my mother for never giving up on God, her husband, or her marriage.

By the time my mother found out she was pregnant with her fourth child, my parents were already rearing two girls and one boy. My mother admits she longed for a second son and had already chosen his name: Jack, after her only brother. At the time Jack, was away fighting in World War II. The idea of passing on Jack's name to her own child somehow eased her fear that she would lose her brother in the war.

Several inches of snow blanketed the ground on the blustery morning of January 16, 1946—the day my mother knew it was time to get to the hospital. We lived about fifteen miles from the Red River County Hospital in Clarksville, Texas. My father bundled up my mother, hitched the wagon, and drove the team of horses through the snow and bone-chilling cold to the closest town, Avery, where he borrowed my aunt's car so they could drive to Clarksville. Because of the snow, the trip took about two hours. They say I came out screaming and kicking, and of course, I wasn't a boy! My mother settled on Jackie for a girl's name. The moment my father saw me, all wet and wrinkled, he cried, "Thank God we have another girl!"

Greeting me when I arrived home from the hospital were squeals of delight from my big sisters—Barbara, who was eight years old, and Marita, who was six—and my big brother, four-year-old Don. They thought it was wonderful to have baby Jackie in the house! I'm told a day didn't go by that my sister Marita didn't kiss me. An older lady once told her, "If you'll kiss baby Jackie every day, then she'll always be happy." And so she did. It must have worked, because I have many happy childhood memories.

In my earliest memories I can see myself sitting close to my father on cool summer evenings, and I hear his soothing voice telling me that from the first time he laid eyes on me he knew I was special. I've always figured that was because I was born after he became a Christian. From the time I was knee-high, he took every opportunity to tell me how the Lord spoke to his heart the day I was born, telling him that I was going to grow up to serve the Lord. Although I didn't understand what all that meant at the time, it made me feel very happy and loved.

Growing up in the country taught me many things about the ways of God. My father was a sharecropper, which simply meant that we farmed on someone else's land in exchange for a share of the produce. Avery, the tomato capitol of northeast Texas, was a farmer's dream with its rich and fertile soil. My father raised tomatoes, cucumbers, and any other vegetable he could sell. That's how we made our living. But even when the crops failed and we had little or no cash payment for the landowner, we had enough to eat. My mother toiled all summer long, canning vegetables from her garden until the shelves in our storm shelter were lined with every size jar containing every vegetable imaginable. Hand-churned butter, fresh eggs, bacon, and sausage were staple foods on the farm. We ate it all whether we liked it or not.

Texas weather is unpredictable, and we considered ourselves fortunate as long as the weather didn't take the cows, the pigs, or the chickens. In those times I learned to be thankful for the things we did have. Isn't it just like the Lord to stagger the seasons of His crops and make them different so food is always available? God provided sausage one winter when we weren't able to rely on our crops. I'm not talking about the neat, lean packages of sausage we have today; I'm talking about pork sausage made into little patties, deep fried in fat, stacked into sterilized jars, and sealed with all the grease poured over them. Our food was all gone, and all we had to eat for several days was this fried sausage. Out of necessity, I learned to thank God for things I didn't like.

More times than I can count I have prayed I Thessalonians 5:18, which reads, "Give thanks in all circumstances, for this is God's will for you in Christ Jesus." Our family learned this valuable lesson, and I've carried that lesson with me to this day.

Even from the times of drought I have many wonderful memories. Some of my fondest memories were of spending the night with Big Mama in her big feather bed. I remember thinking every little girl should be able to sleep beside her grandmother on a fluffy feather bed. I especially liked to steal her wad of chewed gum off the coffee table or countertop or wherever she happened to leave it for later. When the coast was clear, I'd stick the big wad of chewed gum into my mouth and chomp to my heart's delight until every last bit of sugar was gone! I understand why people say stolen water is sweeter. At least, that was the case with stolen gum.

The only grandfather I knew was actually my great-grandfather, Papa Colvins, who was Big Mama's father. My father lost his own dad when I was a small child. His father had been slopping the hogs when he suffered a massive stroke and collapsed in the pigsty. By the time he was found, the pigs had eaten part of his body. His bizarre death left me confused and afraid. And from then on, I stayed away from pigs.

I loved Papa Colvins dearly. He had a handlebar mustache and always wore neatly creased dress pants with suspenders and black boots. I don't believe I ever saw him leave the house without his fashionable gray hat, creased to perfection. I admired the way he took care of himself, always trying to look his best.

I have fond memories of sitting beside Papa while he smoked his favorite pipe. We'd watch wrestling on his little black-and-white television set. I'd sit as still as I could, chewing my stolen gum and breathing in the sweet smell of cherry-scented tobacco. I didn't dare say a word, because Papa was serious about those wrestling matches! I'd sit as quiet as a mouse beside his recliner, listening to him whoop and holler. At those times, I could have sworn Papa and I were the only two people on earth.

The taste of fresh milk in the morning. The smell of my mother's fried chicken on Sunday afternoons, mingling with the sweet aroma of Evening in Paris perfume from the local dime store. Cool, starry nights nestled between my parents. The chirping of crickets in the open country. Sleeping on Big Mama's feather bed. These are fond memories that I will hold in my heart forever.

Life was meant to be perfect. But it never is.

"Explain this!" I demanded after waking my husband up from a nap to show him a matchbook I'd found in his shirt pocket. Ironically, it was a matchbook from the same nightclub where we met and fell in love years earlier. Inside the cover was scribbled another woman's name and phone number.

The next thing I knew his open hand flew toward my face. My cheek throbbed with an intense, stinging pain where he had slapped me. I forced myself to ignore my aching face as profanity spewed from his mouth like lava from a volcano. He blamed me for his unhappiness, by now a familiar accusation, and told me I was a paranoid, untrusting, foolish woman. Paranoid maybe, untrusting definitely, but no longer a fool.

And then it happened. He said the words I couldn't bear to hear a fourth time: "I'm leaving for good!" A thousand knives pierced my stomach. Rage welled up in the spaces shock had created.

"Who will raise the children?" I asked angrily, tears stinging my eyes.

"I'll get a maid," he said matter-of-factly. "When I find a place I'll send for them—for my children, anyway."

As he turned his back on me and walked toward the front door, I knew two things: First, I was not indispensable to him, as I had led myself to believe. He didn't need me, even if I had offered to bring up his children as my own. Second, I knew his threat to leave me was no bluff. The thought of being abandoned with five young children was too much to handle.

I stopped crying, walked to the bedroom and picked up the pistol I swore I would use only in self-defense. And in a way, this was self-defense. I was defending my dignity, regaining what had been stolen all those times I had been beaten, kicked and belittled. This time I was fighting back.

My hand shook as I aimed the trigger.

The first shot went over his shoulder and shattered a picture on the wall. I don't know where the next one ended up, but I remember the look in my husband's eyes as he turned around. It was the same look I had seen in my first husband's eyes—and my second husband's—just before their fists had broken up my face.

I closed my eyes and pulled the trigger a third time. The shot echoed throughout the room. I opened my eyes and saw my husband lying face down, unmoving. The back of his shirt was soaked in blood. Slowly blood began to ooze, forming a dark-red puddle on the hardwood floor.

I walked over, knelt down, put the pistol to the side of his head and asked, "Did you dance with her?"

I planned to kill him on the spot if he dared to answer *yes.*

Chapter Two

Mysterious Woman

The crisp summer night was filled with a million stars flickering like diamonds in the sky. The woman who stood before me glowed like an angel surrounded by God's awesome creation. Something radiant and majestic beamed from her as she raised her hands toward heaven. I fixed my eyes on this mysterious woman, and I knew right away she had something I wanted. From that night on, I wanted to be like Sister Saxton when I grew up.

Growing up poor made me hungry for a better way of life. As a small child, I learned early on that like most of our neighbors, we were definitely not rich. We didn't have indoor plumbing, and washing clothes was an all-day affair. My mother scrubbed the clothes on a washboard after stirring them in a big pot of boiling, lye-soap water in the backyard. We later moved up to a wringer washing machine that took some of the hard labor out of the job. We couldn't afford to buy fabric, so my mother designed her own patterns and made clothes for us out of flour sacks.

Our family made the most out of anything and everything we were given. We were perched on life's break-even point so often that it became a way of life. A family like ours had nothing and no one to depend on for our daily bread other than the hand of God. At any time, the little we had could vanish with the wind-blown soil, and sometimes it did. Proverbs 15:17 says this: "Better a meal of vegetables where there is love than a fattened calf with hatred." The love in our home made up for the years of drought—and greasy sausage patties.

My father would spend many weekends fishing, and he'd often bring home a huge catch of fish. While he cleaned the catch of the day, I meticulously picked through the scales, looking for the right shape and size to make fake fingernails. Carefully, I held my scaly treasures in my cupped hand as if they were gold nuggets. When we arrived home I wasted no time laying them in order of nail size. I used homemade paste to attach them one by one to my own nails. It would be years before artificial nails were invented. How I wished I had patented my fake nails and used them to bring prosperity to our family!

We didn't have toilet paper, so we wiped with the only thing we had available, like magazine pages. My sister Marita taught me how to make paper dolls from catalogue models, and I rescued many beautiful women from the pages of the Sears mail-order catalogues that were routinely stacked in the outhouse. I spent hours alone with my paper dolls, drifting into an imaginary world of glamour and fame, pretending to be a model or a movie star.

My fantasies periodically spilled over into my real world, like the time I pretended to be a world-renowned ballerina. Oh, I imagined myself as a grand ballet dancer, twirling and leaping gracefully through the air. I didn't know that there were special shoes that allowed you to stand on your toes when you danced. I managed, instead, to learn to stand on the tips of a pair of little black flats—for moments on end, poised like a graceful swan.

One day I decided to perform in front of my parents' friends, Mr. and Mrs. Baron. I was in such a hurry to do my ballet routine that I didn't bother to put on shoes or socks. I began to twirl and dance and jump. Suddenly, Mr. Baron cried out, "Chicken toes, chicken toes! Jackie has chicken toes!" My brother and sisters laughed and laughed, and he laughed, and Mrs. Baron laughed, and my mother and father laughed. The whole world seemed to laugh at me. I could feel the blood drain from my face as I stopped in mid-air to look down at my feet. It was true. I had long, skinny toes that looked like a chicken's toes. In a split second, my self-image changed completely. For the first time, I knew what emotional pain and self-loathing felt like.

My father had a smorgasbord of endearing nicknames for me. One was little bird legs. Well, if you combine bird legs with chicken toes, what you get is not a pretty picture! I began wearing thick bobby socks so my ankles would look fat. I wanted to have fat legs so badly that I combed magazines looking for fat pills to order. I'd tell myself, *I'm gonna have fat legs, pretty fat legs, and fat feet!*

Unfortunately, my efforts to get fat were useless, and so I ended my dancing career and stuck to singing. I'd sing all the time. I'd sing to my father when he'd take the vegetables to be sold. I remember him saying, "You're just like a little dime-store radio. I can turn you on, but you can't be turned off!" Then he'd laugh and say, "Sing to me!" So I'd sing and sing and sing.

Singing became my life. In fact, it was a song that made the deepest spiritual impression on my heart when I was a child. I like to think that God knew well in advance that I would need something to give me hope when life's journey became almost too much to bear. For me, it was a song sung by a traveling female evangelist named Sister Saxton.

One starry summer evening Sister Saxton held an old-time revival meeting at our church. Something about the way she spoke and moved reminded me of an angel. She may have worn a plain cotton dress for all I remember now, but to my eyes she was clothed in God's glory. I never saw such a radiance surround a person before—or since, for that matter. Her words were as clear as the stars on the black sky.

When she finished her sermon she sank to her knees, clasped her hands together in prayer and looked up to the heavens as she sang the most beautiful song I've ever heard. The words have become my lifelong prayer:

"I'd like to kneel down and talk it all over with Him.

I'd like to say, Lord, You loved me when the path was so dim.

But I cannot repay Him till I meet Him in the city above,

But I'd like to talk it over and thank Him for His wonderful love."

The song stirred something so deep inside of me that I wanted to talk it over with Jesus just as Sister Saxton had sung about. I wanted to be someone who told others about Jesus. It was as though something pierced my soul, and I said to myself, "I want to be just like Sister Saxton when I grow up."

Eventually my childhood hopes and dreams of being like Sister Saxton were buried beneath a sea of unforgiveness. My once-soft, childlike heart was full of bitterness and rage hardened by years of abuse. I had only myself to blame for my choices in men and my hardness toward God. By the time I was twenty years old, I saw myself as a used-up woman hardened by years of abuse. I didn't see how God could ever find anything worthwhile in me.

Chapter Three

First Love

The winners of the school popularity contest were announced. I was voted most beautiful, and Chuck was voted most handsome. I felt like a fairy-tale princess standing arm in arm with Prince Charming as we were presented to the student body. Time stood still when I glanced at him and he grinned back at me. Cameras snapped. Today, the faded photograph of the beautiful cheerleader and star basketball player is nothing more than a painful reminder of a lost childhood.

Being the baby in the family definitely had its advantages. Unlike my brother and sisters, who worked tirelessly, few demands—if any—were placed on me. Because I was a fair-skinned child, my mother made a point of telling anyone and everyone to keep me out of the sun so my skin wouldn't blister. While the hot Texas sun glared down on my working family, I sat under a giant shade tree happily playing with dolls or chasing the dog.

My brother and sisters worked right alongside my parents until their clothes were drenched in sweat and their

17

hands were callused. But I never lifted a finger. Only on those rare days when the blazing sun hid behind a blanket of clouds was I called on to lend a hand. Even then I felt woozy and faint, so my mother would plop me on a cotton sack and pull me along while she worked.

For me, the back of a cotton sack was a wonderful place to grow up. Unfortunately, my work ethic carried over to the inside of the house. "Go on out and play, Jackie," I was told. "Mother, could you please tell Jackie to get out of the kitchen?" my sisters begged. My sisters never failed to shoo me away, because my efforts at helping were more trouble than they were worth. My siblings did, however, make time for me after the chores were done.

While my sisters spent hours cooking or doing other household chores, I unleashed my imagination and entered my fantasy world until supper was ready or the cleaning was done. The beautiful models in the catalogues—whose photos were now my paper dolls—made such an impression on me that I routinely applied lipstick I "borrowed" from my sister and pinched my cheeks until they were as rosy as a model's.

Now, standing next to Chuck, my world seemed as rich and satisfying as the fantasy world I had created with my paper dolls. My dream of being a real-life beauty became a reality once the votes had been counted. Clumps of glitter sparkled from the shaky backdrop on the stage where we stood, while the other girls looked wistfully at me. I had fulfilled the dream of every girl there—even if I did have chicken toes.

Chuck and I began dating and married a year later. I was fifteen years old, and Chuck was a mature man of nineteen. I was madly in love. No amount of reasoning could convince me that I wasn't ready for a serious commitment. My father had married my mother when she was fifteen years old, and all I wanted was to have a marriage like my parents'. They were happy and in love.

I had it all figured out. As long as I looked pretty and acted sweet and submissive toward my man, that would be enough to carry us through life. Never mind that I didn't know diddly-squat about cooking, cleaning, or sex. And of course, I was clueless about all the emotional baggage individuals often bring into marriage: feelings of rejection, fear, and low self-esteem, all of which are potentially detrimental to any relationship.

I was bound and determined to do things my way, even if it meant going against my parents' and teachers' wishes to wait and marry after I graduated from high school. But I didn't like school, and I didn't see any need to continue. I never felt as if I was "book smart," so marriage seemed the obvious choice for my life.

The wedding took place July 3, 1961, the summer after I completed my sophomore year of high school. I wore a beautiful baby blue street-length chiffon dress, and a full skirt. We were married at a neighbor's house with a few friends and family members attending. The ceremony was short and sweet. After exchanging our vows—for better or worse, for richer or poorer, in sickness and in health—we kissed. And that was that.

The first night of our honeymoon my happily-ever-after dream began to crumble. We pulled up to a motel on a stretch of highway cluttered with beer joints and gas stations just over the state line in Oklahoma. Neon arrows pointed us to the office where we registered and got the key to our room. The minute we stepped into our room I wanted to burst into tears. The room smelled musty, and the bed creaked when I sat on it. Cracks and water stains covered the paper-thin walls, and the bathroom was minuscule. Suddenly, my dreams of romance and passion melted into a sea of disappointment.

Although I was in love, for an instant I wanted to be a little girl again, playing with my paper dolls with all the time in the world to daydream about marriage and children. But my childhood was gone. I'd chosen to make my bed at the age of fifteen, and now I had to lie in it.

In some ways my childhood had been over for several years. It's hard to say exactly when it slipped away, but I know that it left much earlier for me than it did for other girls my age. For one thing, my body began to change into that of a woman when I was ten years old. I think I went to sleep one night as a flat-chested little girl and woke up the next morning with fully developed breasts.

We attended the Lone Pine Baptist Church in Avery for many years. My father had helped build the church and felt a loyalty to it. From the moment I walked down the narrow aisle to accept Jesus as my Savior, I wanted to tell others about the Lord.

A traveling evangelist named Bill Robertson had invited our youth group to go street witnessing in De Kalb, Texas. Now this was a town that had made its mark on the map: It was the home of Dan Blocker, one of the stars of the television show *Bonanza*. You couldn't go anywhere without hearing that bit of trivia. De Kalb's other claim to fame was that Elvis had performed in the town square. My heart pounded with excitement as our little band of Christian soldiers made its way to the hub of this small east Texas town.

We sat in the back of a panel truck and circled the town square, waving banners as Brother Bill shouted "Jesus saves!" into a megaphone. Recorded music blared through speakers. I'm sure every lost—and saved—soul heard our message. I just don't think anyone got saved that day. We never actually talked to anyone or tried to find out the needs of the community. Our job was easy; the big loudspeaker and recorded music did most of the work. Boy, was it exciting.

The same year I gave my heart to Jesus was the same year my mother convinced my father to stop farming and move to Lubbock, Texas, to work in a cotton mill. The cotton business was booming, and my mother was tired of living from crop to crop. My father plunged headfirst into his new job at the mill, preparing the cotton to be baled. It was no sooner that he had begun working that he injured his back.

My father's injury turned out to be both a blessing and a curse. The blessing came when he received a settlement from the owners of the mill that allowed us to move back to Avery. We even had enough money to put down on our first *real* home.

Somewhere along that road from Lubbock back to Avery, I changed from a lanky girl with oversized breasts into a proportionally developed young woman. People could hardly believe I was the same girl. Boys tripped over themselves to get my attention.

The tide continued to shift when I was chosen to be a cheerleader. For the first time in my life, I felt as if I belonged. I adored the attention I got as I jumped and yelled in front of the fans that filled the small stadium. I would really fix myself up; I had the makeup and hair thing down pat, and I knew just how to smile to please the world.

Slowly, my desire for popularity began to replace my desire for God. I let other people's opinions of me replace my hunger and thirst for God's approval. Oh, you'd never know it by looking at me. I was in church every time the doors were open, but the seeds of rebellion had slowly begun to take root. I began to trust myself over my parents and God.

In high school, it didn't take long for Chuck to become my world. I thought about him night and day. After all, it had been love at first sight. At over six feet tall, he made me feel safe when I rested my head on his broad shoulder. But what I remember most were his eyes. They were sky blue, accented by a thick layer of long, black, curly lashes that sat heavy on the tips of his eyelids, giving his eyes a sleepy, dreamy look. And the first time he kissed me, my heart raced.

The cheerleader and the school basketball star. The most beautiful girl and the most handsome boy. It was a match made in heaven.

My parents didn't think so. They saw our blossoming romance from a different perspective. They knew how hard it was to be married so young, with no education, always struggling to make ends meet. They wanted to spare me the hardship they knew I'd face.

One night I couldn't stand it any longer. I had to tell Chuck that I loved him and wanted to get married. In the middle of the night, I slipped out of the house and began walking down Route 82 toward Chuck's house. A truck driver pulled over and gave me a lift for the last few miles. He fussed at me and lectured me about being out alone on a major highway where anything could happen to me. But I didn't pay attention. Seeing Chuck was the only thing on my mind.

I reached his house and found my way to his bedroom window. "Chuck...Chuck," I whispered, tapping the windowpane lightly.

Chuck stirred and opened his eyes to see my face at his window. "What are you doing?" he asked, half-asleep.

He opened the window, and I crawled into his room. I paused to catch my breath. "Chuck...I just had to tell you that

I'm in love with you, and I want to get married!" I whispered excitedly.

I'm sure he thought I'd lost my mind, coming over in the middle of the night to tell him something he already knew. Finally, he agreed to marry me.

"Someday," he promised.

I was afraid my father would change his mind when the big day finally arrived and he went to the courthouse to sign the papers giving his consent. I perspired every step of the way until the pen touched the paper. Then we made it official. Chuck and I were married.

Now my stomach knotted up as I stared at the stained ceiling. *What am I doing here?* my thoughts screamed.

I don't know what I was expecting. Maybe candles. Romantic music. Fireworks. Cinderella marries Prince Charming. It was all a big disappointment. The little I did know about sex I had learned in the backseat of Chuck's car. I wasn't even sure how a girl got pregnant. I had so many questions, but I was too afraid to ask my mother.

In the early 1960s sex education was unheard of, and talk shows weren't around to provide their brand of education. Sex was a taboo subject, at least between most parents and their children. Kids in rural areas learned about sex from watching farm animals mate and give birth.

I was naive and afraid. Suddenly, I wanted to be asleep in my own bed with my parents in the next room. The sound of trucks whizzing by all night only intensified my misery in that motel room with its thin, cracked walls and lopsided bed. Even my imagination couldn't rescue me from the painful reality that I had married too young.

Exposed Heart

I rolled over on my side and stared at my sleeping husband. Tears streamed down my face, but I was careful not to make a sound.

Chapter Four

Shattered Dreams

My dream was a simple one: a small house with a white picket fence and a gate that opened and closed to keep an evil world at bay. Laughing, healthy children to fill the empty rooms. A husband to hold me close at night. What more could a girl want in life? And yet, my real and make-believe worlds were never to meet. Reality haunted me in the night as I lay in bed—sore from the beatings, my bruised heart crying out to be loved. Like a fading picture my dreams slowly began to die.

After our honeymoon was over, Chuck began working at an ammunition plant about thirty miles from Avery, and we rented a small apartment nearby. Chuck worked hard to make enough money to pay the rent and put food on the table.

It was no secret that Chuck resented being married. When I looked into his eyes I saw a man who missed his old life. I couldn't blame him for his feelings. He was fresh out of high school, spending his summer knee-deep in a lifestyle he didn't want. I tried not to think about it, but I felt guilty because I knew my impatience had caused me to pressure him into getting married. *Someday* wasn't good enough for me. I wanted to be married as soon as possible, and neither hell nor high water could have stopped me.

For better or for worse. Our wedding vows echoed inside my head. Reciting our vows over and over again was my way of being reassured that no matter how tough things got, we would stick it out. My hopes soon dwindled. Chuck began to spend more time at the local bar, drinking and cutting up with his new friends. It hurt deeply to admit to myself that Chuck would rather be out with his buddies than at home with me.

I waited for the perfect moment to share my feelings. When the time felt right, I broke the silence. "I love you, Chuck. And I know you love me. So why can't we spend more time together in the evenings? Your buddies get you all day at work. It doesn't seem fair for them to take your evenings too," I pleaded.

Chuck's piercing eyes sent a shiver down my spine. "Hey, I don't need this right now. I think I deserve some understanding for all I do for you. I work all day so you can have a place to live and food to eat. And all you can do is nag, nag, nag," he said.

I choked back the tears. The words I wanted to say were caught in the back of my throat. Chuck seemed to notice my anguish, and his voice softened. "It's no big deal, really," he explained. "We drink a few beers, and that's it." He slipped his arm around my waist. "You don't have anything to worry about," he assured me.

The more I thought about it, the more I realized Chuck was right. I expected too much. It wasn't fair for Chuck not to have time with his friends. I felt stupid and ashamed of my worries and fears. My needs were selfish.

He needed a place to unwind after a grueling workday, not a lecture from me. I decided to never complain again. And yet, the pain and jealousy stayed with me.

My fairy-tale world died somewhere between "Once upon a time…" and "…they lived happily ever after." I was no longer an imaginary princess swept away by my knight in shining armor. I was a fifteen-year-old girl desperately trying to protect my marriage at any cost. As the lonely months crept along I became obsessed with being the perfect wife. I spent almost every waking moment trying to please the man I loved more than anything in the world.

Two months after we were married, I found out I was pregnant. This didn't seem to bother Chuck at all. However, we were both so young and needy, and considering the other issues at work in our lives, we were in no position to deal with having a baby. But abortion did not even enter my mind; it was simply not an option. My growing nausea, the changes in my body, and the realization that I was becoming a mother fueled my insecurities. And I was spoiled. I wanted a lot of attention, and I wasn't getting it. I felt alone and abandoned and rejected.

The more I nagged the more possessive and dominating he became. We both felt trapped. I didn't have a car or a job. I was stuck in a tiny, cramped apartment all day long with very little to do except dream about the two of us growing old together with children running through the house and a dog in the backyard. That's how I kept myself going when my circumstances looked bleak and daunting.

My sole purpose in life was to make Chuck happy. It was my job. My happiness depended on it. One time I spent an entire day preparing the best meal I could think to cook. It was a meal my mother had prepared my whole life: fried pork chops, beans, corn bread, tomatoes, and iced tea. It was my first attempt at cooking a big meal, and much of it involved guesswork since my mother wasn't there to show me how to do everything.

Every hair was in place and my makeup was done just right when Chuck arrived home. I was standing outside the door anxiously waiting for him in a pretty pink cotton maternity dress. I imagined Chuck embracing me with hugs and kisses. Perhaps he would whisk me off to the bedroom overcome with excitement and passion. I settled on the front porch to wait for my husband.

The tires hit the gravel driveway. The car door slammed, and I sat in disbelief as Chuck stormed past me without saying a word. I followed him into the house like a puppy dog, my hopes for a romantic evening dissipating as each second passed by. Despair and disbelief draped me like a heavy cloak. "What's wrong?" I whimpered.

Without any warning he backhanded me across the face. "I know what you're doing! You were out there trying to show off for people passing by!" he shouted.

Tears welled up in my eyes, and I blinked hard to keep from crying. My cheek felt hot from the blow. "That was the farthest thing from my mind!" I cried. "I was only waiting to meet you when you came home to tell you how much I've missed you and how I couldn't wait to see you!"

I followed him into the kitchen, wounded, hoping that the sight of supper would change his mood. I knew that my cooking wasn't as good as my mother's, and I had a horrible feeling that the beans were too salty. However, by my feeble standards it was the biggest and best meal I'd ever cooked.

Chuck sat down without a word. He took one spoonful of the beans. In a whirlwind of fury he threw his plate against the wall. The next thing I knew, every dish that I had painstakingly prepared was on the floor or on the wall or both.

Hot tears ran from my eyes. My lips quivered.

Without a word, Chuck stormed out of the house and didn't return until sometime in the early hours of the morning. I cleaned up the spilled food and broken dishes, and blamed myself for his outburst. The beans were too salty, I decided.

It didn't take long for this form of abuse to become a ritual whenever I cooked something he didn't like. And then there were other reasons for his outbursts. Saying the wrong thing could make him explode with anger. If I looked at him the wrong way, he'd slap the fire out of me.

After each explosion of anger, Chuck's fury would subside like the calm after a storm. He'd hold me close and rub my bulging stomach. "I love you, Jackie. I swear to God I never meant to hurt you. I love you. I'd give my life for you and the baby. I'll never hurt you again," he promised.

Until I was married, abuse was foreign to me. I didn't understand why the abuse kept happening. The only time I'd ever seen this sort of violent behavior was when one of my uncles beat up his girlfriend. My father intervened, because it happened in our home. It crushed me to admit that my uncle, my hero, was an abusive man. But never in a million years did I think any man would abuse me in the same way.

It wasn't long before the abuse escalated to terrifying proportions. One night Chuck had been out later than usual. "Where have you been?" I demanded.

Without warning he yanked a pillow from our bed and pressed it over my face, crushing my head and shoulders into the mattress. I clawed at him and tried to push the pillow away so I could breathe. I wrestled for my life as I fought for oxygen. It seemed like an eternity before he removed the pillow. I sat up, choking and gasping for air. Afterwards I told myself, *If I could just be a better wife, or if I could just hold my tongue and not argue back, or if I would just do something right he wouldn't get so mad at me. It's got to be my fault somehow.*

Most of the abuse occurred after he'd been drinking, and it worsened as the months crept slowly by. Each explosion of rage was more horrible than the one before. Many times I'd think, *This is it...I'm going to die this time!* I not only feared for my life but also for the life of my unborn baby.

I'd always heard that pregnant women were the most beautiful, but the body I saw in the mirror told me otherwise. The sleepless nights I spent worrying about my marriage had taken a toll on me. My legs, feet, and ankles swelled up like balloons. I may have wanted fat ankles as a little girl, but this was definitely not what I had in mind.

I looked haggard and tired, and our sex life dwindled to nothing. I was beginning to suspect that Chuck was seeing other women. I could never prove anything, though. If I dared to voice my suspicions, I was immediately quieted with a slap to my face.

The labor pains started one Sunday afternoon. The whole family drove me to a hospital in Clarksville. My doctor had been in practice for forty years, and he didn't believe in Caesarian deliveries. He was a country doctor who believed birthing a baby was as natural as a cow giving birth to a calf.

After thirty-six hours of grueling labor, I cried from sheer exhaustion and joy when I heard the faint whimper of my newborn son. I was sixteen years old when he was born. My life felt complete as I looked down at his beautiful face. Chuck and I named him Michael David.

I hoped that having a baby would solve the problems in our marriage, but the arguments and abuse continued. My pride would never let me admit to anyone that I didn't have a perfect life, especially since my sisters' marriages seemed to be working out well.

Six months after Mike was born, I became pregnant with a second child. This time I gave birth to a beautiful daughter. We named her Charlsey after her daddy. I called her my little baby doll.

My life was finally perfect. A little boy, a little girl, and a husband who sometimes acted as if he loved me. I had hope. Once again I thought, *Now my life will be happy. Now we can put our problems behind us and have a happy family.*

For a brief time things seemed to be better. Chuck quit his job at the ammunition plant and found a carpentry job. We moved to an apartment on the outskirts of Dallas.

When Mikey was three years old, he was diagnosed with cerebral palsy. The doctor said the condition was caused by the restricted flow of oxygen to his brain as he made an unusually slow descent through the birth canal. Waves of anguish and disappointment swept through me like the ebb and flow of the ocean tide. "If only" became a form of self-abuse. *If only I had insisted on a Caesarian section, my baby would be all right. If only God had protected my baby...*

Life went from bad to worse after Mike's diagnosis. One night Chuck didn't come home at all. I found some phone numbers tucked inside his dresser drawer and began to call them one by one. I didn't sleep all night as I thought about ways to trap him in what I knew was an ugly lie. Early the next morning, a girl's voice confirmed my worst fear.

"Is Chuck there?" I asked.

"Sorry, he went with the guys to get some more beer. Who is this?" she asked.

My mind went blank. "Uh, I'm a friend of Chuck's," I said in a matter-of-fact tone. "Where are you? I want to come over and party with y'all."

She gave me the address, and I arranged for my children to stay with a neighbor. I immediately headed on foot to the location I'd been given. Wearing a new pair of high-heeled shoes and a matching outfit, I began the treacherous walk to find my husband.

I was weak and exhausted. I didn't have a car or any money for a cab. But my rage and jealousy fueled my weary body with the burst of energy I needed to make the long walk. I remember how frightening it was walking along that highway, but I was determined to catch him, to see with my own eyes that he was cheating on me. My feet were blistered and ached so badly that eventually I was forced to hitch a ride. When I got to the apartment, I discovered that Chuck hadn't returned yet. But the evidence was all there. Crushed beer cans were scattered everywhere. A half-naked, drunken girl, cursing like a sailor, greeted me with tales about the great time she'd had the night before. She bragged about how she'd slept with Chuck.

I clenched my fists, and my jaw tightened. My thoughts screamed, *I hate her! I hate Chuck! I hate my life!*

I left and made my way back to the busy highway to hitch a ride home. I had all the proof I needed. After Chuck figured out that I had been to the apartment, he phoned me. "I swear, I never had sex with her," he lied. "You're an idiot for trying to embarrass me in front of my friends!"

It amazed me the way he could flip a story around to make me look like the bad guy. And I began to believe that the whole thing was my fault, not his. I deserved to be beaten.

I took my punishment, in front of the children. And I continued to take it for several weeks. My feet continued to ache. Sometimes the pain was so unbearable that I couldn't walk. Finally, I went to the doctor. He told me I had a bone spur caused by walking in high heels for such a long distance. He also said I was dangerously underweight.

But the visit didn't end there. He began asking questions about my life, questions no one had ever asked me before.

For the first time, I told the truth. I felt safe in the doctor's office, and I broke down in tears. I told him about the attempted suffocation, the beatings, the other women. It was as if someone pulled the cork and my feelings gushed out. I couldn't stop the flow of words, nor did I want to.

He looked me square in the eyes and said sternly, "If you stay in this situation it's going to kill you. You have to leave, for your safety and your children."

No one had ever told me that leaving was an option. But then I'd never opened up to anyone before. Hearing those words made me genuinely fear for my life.

When the ashes of my life had settled, I was nineteen years old and in a situation that forced me to face the consequences of my rebellion. Chuck and I had both been too young and immature to take on the responsibility of a marriage. The seeds of rejection had borne the fruit of loneliness, despair, and bitterness. My life was in ruins. My children needed to be someplace safe, away from the daily violence their innocent eyes had seen.

And so I left.

While Chuck was at work I packed my belongings and took the children to my parents' house. Unknowingly, I carried even more baggage than I thought—a truckload of fear, hurt, anger, and rejection that would resurface in each of my future marriages. But at the time I didn't know that. All I knew was that my Prince Charming had turned out to be a man full of anger and resentment, and somehow I was at fault.

I closed the door behind me and never looked back.

Chapter Five

Restless Heart

The train pulled up at the station. I boarded with my two children, ages three and four, one in each arm. Minneapolis promised a fresh start and a future of some kind. Exactly what that future was, I didn't know. The only thing that mattered was that we were free from the past. For the first time since my wedding day there would be no more heartache, no more fear, no more pain. I'd been given a second chance to find happiness.

A blast of frigid air caught me off guard as I got off the train and scurried toward the station, where my sister and brother-in-law were waiting. I felt pretty wearing my three-quarter-length suede coat with the mink collar. I wore no gloves, boots or other accessories essential for twenty-below-zero weather. In the fancy high-heeled shoes that matched my new dress, I was ready for the big city—or so I thought.

My sister Marita and her husband, Mickey, greeted us with warm hugs and kisses, which helped take the edge off the bone-chilling weather. By the time I reached the car my fingers were frozen and stiff, like icicles dangling from my hands. I had no feeling in my feet. My face stung as the wind whipped my face like a leather strap. I didn't care. My heart pounded with excitement as I imagined a fresh start.

It didn't take long for the kids and me to adjust to our new surroundings. Charlsey formed a special relationship with her Aunt Marita. She followed my sister around the house chattering nonstop about anything that could possibly enter a three-year-old's mind. On the other hand, Mike, whom I affectionately called Mikey, continued to trail others his age in verbal and motor skills. His sweet disposition made up for his handicap. Sometimes I'd scoop him up in my arms and hold him tight while Charlsey stole kisses from him. As hard as life had been for my children, I still thanked the Lord for giving them to me. They were all I had, and I wanted them safe and happy.

I'll be forever grateful to Marita and Mickey for caring enough to overlook my mistakes and to take us into their home. I wish I had listened to her before all this happened and had not been so bullheaded in my ways.

As the days and weeks ran together I became more discontent with my dependence on my sister and brother-in-law. I wanted a place of my own. I could not shake the feeling that I needed to be independent. But this meant getting a job to pay for groceries, childcare, and rent.

Over the course of my life I had answered to my parents, my husband, and now my sister and brother-in-law. I made up my mind that I was going to find a job and make it on my own.

I obtained my first job by lying about my age. A waitress had to be at least twenty-one years old to work in a restaurant where alcohol was served. At nineteen, I couldn't afford to wait two years. I had no high school degree and no job experience.

How hard could it be? I asked myself. *Writing down what customers want to eat and putting the food down in front of them is no big deal.*

I remember dressing up and putting on a cute little hat for my job interview. I looked the restaurant manager square in the eyes and lied like a dog. "I'm twenty-one," I told him.

"Have you worked in a restaurant before?" he asked.

"Yes, sir," I answered confidently.

He hired me on the spot.

My first day at work was a living nightmare. People sat down faster than I could serve them. As soon as I'd bring glasses of water to one table, another group would sit down. My brain ached as I scribbled down orders while the other waiters whizzed around me. The room became a blur of chaos and confusion. I wanted to cry.

I recall one group of about six or seven businessmen who sat at a large table in my assigned section of the restaurant. I felt overwhelmed by the time their orders came up. I didn't know who had ordered what. I guess they felt sorry for me, because they left me a nice tip despite my lousy waitressing skills.

My feet ached. My back hurt. I was humiliated by everything that happened that day. I never went back to the restaurant, not even to pick up my paycheck.

Marita, sensing that my spirits needed a boost, helped me find a job at the electronics company where her husband worked as an accountant. I'm sure they had given me a measly little job just to keep me busy, but to this day I don't remember exactly what that job was. However, simply being employed seemed to work, and my self-esteem started to improve.

But rebellion continued to brew inside me. I missed having a man with broad shoulders. I wanted to snuggle in the arms of someone who made me feel petite and feminine. I missed the "don't mess with my woman" attitude that made me feel treasured and secure. I craved the passion that once burned like a fire between Chuck and I. I dreamed of adventure, of romance—the feeling that had enticed me to follow a dream all the way to Minneapolis.

The tension between Marita and me reached a boiling point one night when I went out with my new friends from work. We made plans to meet at a bar in a nearby bowling alley. I was ready for action, and Marita knew it. An all-out verbal war erupted between us. Nobody won. I left the house enraged and more determined than ever to do things my way.

After arriving at the bowling alley, I made a beeline for the bar and planted myself on a stool to wait for my pals. My dyed, blue-black hair, makeup, and tight clothes, combined with the face of a naive, lost young woman searching for love, was all it took. And there he was sitting three stools down from me. Someone to bandage my lonely, aching heart. A stranger to rescue me from all the rules.

And rescue me he did.

The drinks kicked in, and I rattled off my story. "My sister is going to kick me out of the house if I don't do what she tells me to do. She is trying to run my life," I fumed.

I topped the whole story off with the fact that the kids and I had nowhere to go. After a few drinks he was no longer a stranger. I had found someone to rescue me. "Bring your kids and live at my place until you get your feet on the ground," he insisted.

My heart leaped with exhilaration knowing I was free to do my own thing. Lucky me. He was my ticket out. Without a moment's thought I gave way to impulse. "I'll go with you," I said, placing my hand on top of his.

When I arrived home, Marita hit the roof! She accused me of living like a tramp, among other things, and tried to cram some common sense into my thick head, but I didn't listen. "He's got a good-paying job at the television station. He can handle us," I insisted.

"You're making a big mistake," said Marita, shaking her head from side to side. "A big mistake!"

The kids and I moved out the next day. The move was my first step toward taking charge of my life. Freedom was finally within reach.

For a while our living arrangement worked out. He (and I use the word *he* because for the life of me I can't remember his name, even though I lived with him and he supported us for several months) turned out to be a very caring person. At the time it all made sense. It was a perfect arrangement. I had the use of a car, I lived in comfort, and we were all safe. But something...a small something...made me feel dirty inside. The Holy Spirit was convicting me of sin, and I knew it.

I told this guy that I needed to move out for the sake of appearances, so he put us up in a plush hotel that allowed guests to pay by the week. How foolish of me to think that I could somehow ease my conscience by a change of scenery! That was like trying to make a deal with the Holy Spirit: *I'll clean up my act if You'll leave me alone.*

The truth is that sin is sin. And candy-coating sin to make it look like something else is hypocrisy. That is what Jesus meant when He warned the church leaders about living their lives like a cup that looks clean on the outside but is filthy on the inside. In the same way, I found some comfort in being able to honestly say I wasn't *living* with this man. Inwardly, I still felt dirty.

I shut out the unwelcomed feeling and kept right on living in sin. It wasn't long before I met another man who promised me bigger and better things. I met him in the hotel lobby. We kept bumping into one another on the elevator, in the lobby, all around the hotel. My heart melted as I looked into his dark brown eyes. Destiny smiled on me the day I met him—or so I thought.

After a brief romance he promised to whisk me away to a never-never land where I would live the life of a fairy-tale princess. Actually, the land was Iraq, and my fairy-tale prince was a wealthy Middle Eastern businessman who promised me the moon if I'd marry him and move to his country.

Oh, he was beautiful! I know that's not the word one normally associates with a man, but there is no other way to describe him. He was tall, dark, handsome, and rich! How he could fall in love with a silly American teenager, I'll never know. But he insisted that we were meant for each other, and he was willing to care for my children as if they were his own.

I called Marita.

Marita called Mother.

Mother called me.

"We'll never see you or the kids again if you go off with him to his country! He might not let you ever come back!" she pleaded.

As much as I enjoyed the idea of being the bride of a wealthy man in a foreign country, the thought of never seeing my family again scared me away from the whole idea. It sounded like something straight out of a romance novel, except this was real. I knew enough to know that real life doesn't always have a happy ending.

I convinced myself that it sounded too good to be true. And what if my mother was right? All the money, adventure, and "happily ever afters" in the world weren't worth the risk of losing my family.

Much to everyone's relief, I accepted a one-way plane ticket back to Texas to live with my parents. Life in the big city was a closed chapter.

Chapter Six

Born Loser

Autumn arrived with its array of vibrant colors. Gold, red, and yellow leaves drifted to the ground as the fall winds blew. Soon the branches were barren, and the colorful leaves turned brown and died. The winds in my life were also blowing. The exuberance that I had taken to Minneapolis slowly drained out of me. I lost all my passion for life. Almost a year to the day after setting out to find a new life for the kids and myself, I was back at square one with nothing to show for it.

Sunday morning I went to church. This time it was a little Pentecostal church in Avery that we had visited when I was a child. The women wore their long hair tightly wound in a bun on top of their heads. They dressed in drab cotton dresses, with no makeup, no jewelry, and absolutely no heels! The first Sunday I attended church there I made my appearance all dolled up in makeup, jewelry, a stylish dress, and, of course, spike-heeled shoes.

What I remember most about the service was the glorious music. The girl who played the piano sang beautifully. The words and melody penetrated my veins. I wanted to sit on the hard wooden pew for the rest of my life, basking in the Holy Spirit's presence. I thought to myself, *Oh, if I could just sing like that girl I'd be in heaven!*

No sooner had I thought those words than I rose from my seat and made my way to the front of the little country church to give my heart to Jesus for the second time. I had lived a sinful life, and I was ready to do whatever it took to make it right with God.

I readily embraced all the rules from the get-go. I took off the makeup, wore plain cotton dresses that swallowed up my figure, packed away my jewelry, and wore flat, ugly shoes. I exchanged my colorful outfits for something drab and colorless.

I watched the girl pound the piano keys as we belted out song after song to the glory of God. The music let my soul take flight into the heavens where I could soar like an eagle, while the laws and traditions became an anchor for my restless heart.

The euphoria lasted as long as the songs and the sermons did. By mid-week I was back at church for another fix to get me through the rest of the week. The colorless, black-and-white world that I had entered began to choke the life out of me. Not even the music could lift me off the ground, and the rules became like heavy chains around my neck.

Secretly, I began wearing a tad of mascara to make my lashes look thicker and longer. Next, I applied a pale, natural-colored lipstick. Of course, most of the women in the church were much older than I, and at twenty dressing "old" wasn't working for me.

The harder I tried to keep the rules of the church, the more I failed—and the more makeup I applied. Finally, I threw my arms up in frustration and quit going to church. I never doubted that God loved me. I just doubted that He could ever use a failure like me.

My parents were disappointed that I had left the church. My mother urged me to pursue a career in nursing, as she had done when she was a young woman. Whether I liked it or not, I had two small children to support and no husband. At the time her suggestion seemed like the most practical solution to my problem.

At first, the very idea of returning to school terrified me. I wasn't book smart; life had been my school. It took me days to summon the courage to take the high school equivalency test. I passed the GED exam and applied for admission to a nearby junior college. I was ecstatic when I received the news that I had been accepted. My confidence snowballed after that.

Oh, I knew I could do it! *I think I can! I think I can!* soon became *I know I can! I know I can!* It took every morsel of strength and determination inside me to fight for my goal to become a licensed vocational nurse. I knew my dream was within reach!

Day in and day out I made the fifty-mile drive to Texarkana Junior College while my children stayed in day care. I'd failed at everything else. This time the finish line was in sight!

I worked hard at my studies. Most of all I enjoyed the hospital care rotation. I'd bring the patients little cups of juice or water and fluff their pillows. My training introduced me to people who needed help. Loving those patients and making them feel special filled a vacuum inside of me that no man or church service had ever come close to filling. I was caring for people, and it felt right.

One day I read my work order, which instructed me to check on an elderly man's catheter. Well, I read it wrong and thought the instructions said to take his catheter out. I cringe every time I think about yanking that poor man's catheter out without doing it properly!

Another part of my training tested my responses to different situations. One day I was sent to a nursing home. It was seven o'clock in the morning when I walked into the patient's room carrying a food tray. "Good morning," I said cheerfully as I prepared to serve the breakfast.

Suddenly, the elderly patient pulled back the covers revealing the fact that he had not been able to reach the toilet to relieve himself. As I stood there holding the food tray, a wave of nausea swept over me. I thought to myself, *What can I do? I don't think I can handle this!* My hands began to shake, and I became very nauseated!

Running to the nurses' station, I was ordered to return to the patient's room and clean up the mess. "I can't do it," I said.

"It's part of your job training," I was told.

The conversation continued in this manner. The supervisor eventually believed me, so she sent someone else to clean up the mess. I was given another assignment that morning. But my confidence had dwindled to almost nothing.

The last straw came during my final rotation in the emergency room. A doctor instructed me to help hold down a patient who was drunk and had been in a car crash. I turned my head to one side. I hated the sight of blood, and the patient was bleeding profusely. The stench of alcohol was awful. I began to feel dizzy.

I watched the doctor work furiously to stop the flow of blood by tying off the veins in the man's legs. But I couldn't ignore the blood that dripped onto the floor, forming a puddle.

"Doctor, I'm getting sick!" I cried.

Without looking up the doctor replied gruffly, "No, you're not!"

I warned him a second time. "Doctor, I'm getting sick!"

He instructed me to put my head down between my legs. I remember the angry tone in his voice. He was so frustrated with me. The room began spinning. As badly as I wanted to do my job, my stomach wouldn't cooperate. And then everything went black.

I wasn't unconscious very long, because I soon heard the doctor yelling, "Get her out of here! Get her out of here!"

I never went back after that, not even to say good-bye to my teachers or classmates. I was so humiliated. I was only one month away from getting my degree. Once again, I had sabotaged any hope for success in my miserable life.

I've told myself a thousand times I simply wasn't cut out for nursing, which is the truth. I would have been the kind of nurse that nobody would want to have take care of them. But all my reasoning could not repair the damage my short-lived nursing experience did to my self-confidence.

By my own standards I'd failed at everything: marriage, jobs, church, and school. It would be years before I could look in the mirror and see anything other than a born loser.

Chapter Seven

Back in the Saddle

At twenty-one I felt like a used, washed-up old woman. The bags under my eyes from sleepless nights were a stark reminder of the hard road I'd chosen to walk. A part of me wanted to return to the Lord Jesus, but another part of my heart, a bigger part, convinced me that the longing inside my heart could only be filled by a man. I yearned for Mr. Wonderful. Someone to hold me close at night. Someone to wipe away my tears. The clock was ticking, and my chances for happiness were dwindling with each passing day. It was time to find a man and settle down.

Two years later, the abuse at the hands of my first husband was a fading memory, and I was ready to get married again. I carefully steered away from any man who appeared to be as hotheaded as Chuck had been.

I met Fred at a rodeo. He was the rough-and-tumble cowboy type. Fred wore a black cowboy hat, brass belt buckle, ostrich-skin boots, and a smile as big as Texas. I admired his broad shoulders and tight Wrangler jeans. Each time he ran his fingers through his wavy black hair, my heart skipped a beat.

Fred looked like a linebacker. He had a rough, gruff exterior that would scare some women away, but what other women couldn't see were the qualities that drew me to him. Somehow, I knew that beneath his tough cowboy image there was a loving teddy bear waiting for me. My goal was to find it.

My appearance had changed quite a bit after my first marriage. I wore a hairpiece on top of my dyed black hair to give me a big-hair, Texas look. I kept up with the latest fashions, always determined to outdress anyone, anywhere. I wanted to be a showstopper. Inwardly I felt stupid, and I didn't think I had the type of personality that would attract people. I banked on my looks to get attention.

After a whirlwind romance—two weeks to be exact—Fred and I visited a justice of the peace and tied the knot. It's no secret that I married Fred for all the wrong reasons. He had more money than I'd ever dreamed of having. His father owned a large ranch, the kind you see on television. There was something terribly romantic about sitting next to a real-live cowboy in his pickup truck checking on the cattle that grazed on land as far as the eye could see. I married him for security and happiness; love would come later. It was like leaping off a cliff, hoping that somehow I'd land on my feet.

Our wedding night confirmed that I'd made yet another mistake. I had no passion for Fred. I remember thinking, *Oh God, what have I done? I've married a man that I don't love, and now I'm stuck with him for the rest of my life!* I cried silent tears as my new husband slept peacefully beside me. I barely knew this person. I'd married a stranger. Once again my honeymoon fantasy turned into stark reality. The passion and the romance were never there.

I kept my feelings to myself, hoping a miracle would occur and my heart would change. Fred pampered me with gifts and loving embraces. Every day I hoped that *this* would be the day I would fall in love with him.

His father bought us a doublewide trailer that was larger than many houses I'd seen. It was the nicest place I'd ever lived, complete with three large bedrooms, two bathrooms, a large kitchen, and a den. We lived on his father's land, a parcel that was nothing more than a piece of hard, dried pasture where his cattle once grazed until they were moved to greener pastures. I didn't mind not having a yard, and the dried manure piles resembled rocks. With a little imagination, I was like a young bride on one of those old western shows living off the land with a strong man to take care of me.

Two months into our marriage, Fred left to go out of town on a business trip. He told me he'd be gone for a couple of days. I was taken by surprise when he showed up a day earlier than expected. It was a fluke that I even discovered he was back in town. Driving into town to get my hair done, I passed his pickup on the highway. I smiled and waved. Fred, in turn, gave me the middle finger!

I swung the car around and followed him to the trailer. "What's the matter with you?" I asked angrily.

Fred nostrils flared. "You know damn well what you've done!" he snapped.

I rebutted, "Well, no! I don't know what I've done to deserve being flipped off!"

His face turned beet red, and his eyes turned evil. The gentle teddy bear I had married turned into a fierce, ugly beast in front of my eyes. "You know damn well what I'm talking about!" he yelled at the top of his lungs.

"Look," I said calmly, "if you don't apologize, I'll move out."

The veins on his neck swelled; they looked as if they were about to burst. "*Never!*" he thundered.

I stiffened, put my shoulders back, lifted my head up and decided this was my ticket out of a marriage that never should have been. "Well then, I'm leaving!" I declared.

Fred grabbed my arm and yanked me toward him so hard that my neck jolted and pain shot through my arm. The veins in his neck pulsed. His face became redder. It was as if the devil himself looked into my eyes when he sneered, "You'll never leave me...never. I'll kill you if you try. You hear me? You will never leave me!"

His grip tightened around my arm, and I was afraid he was going to break it. Before I could free myself from his crushing grip, he picked me up and threw me out of the trailer. I landed on the hard ground with a thud. I lay on my back and watched in terror as he lunged toward me. His 260 pounds came crashing down on my body.

Fred held my arms down with his knees as he began to punch my face with his clenched fists over and over and over again. I don't believe an inch of my face escaped his fist. He punched my ears, my eyes, my nose, my mouth, my forehead, my cheeks, and my chin as if I was a human punching bag.

Pinned to the ground under his crushing weight, I felt terror grip my heart. The taste of blood mingling with the smell of Fred's sweat made my stomach churn. I kept thinking, *The next blow is it! I'm going to die!*

Bolts of indescribable pain shot through my fragile body, and I couldn't do a thing about it. I was as helpless as an injured deer looking into the barrel of a hunter's rifle. I was certain death was near.

In my heart I cried out, *Please, God! Rescue me! I don't want to die. Please, please, help me get away!*

Somewhere deep inside of me I sensed God's spirit, the Holy Spirit, giving me life-saving words: *Jackie, tell him that you forgive him.*

Without a moment's hesitation I choked out the words, "I forgive you! I forgive you!"

I hated this man with every breath that I had left in me. I couldn't stand the sight or smell of him, and yet I kept saying over and over again that I forgave him.

I could barely see through my swollen eyes, but I felt his body relax as the tension drained out of him. He collapsed on top of me, sobbing and sniffling. His massive body heaved as uncontrollable sobs poured from him. The full weight of his body made it hard for me to breathe, but I didn't dare try to reposition myself. I didn't move a muscle.

Through the muffled cries I could hear him say, "I never meant to hurt you. I love you. I swear I didn't mean to hurt you!"

I waited until the threat of another outburst subsided. "Could you please let me get up so I can take something for my headache?" I asked.

After what seemed like an eternity Fred raised himself off of me. My clothes were soaked from his tears and sweat. The smell disgusted me. I wanted to rip off my clothes and run as far away from him as I could get. But the desire to see my children grow up kept me from doing what I most wanted to do.

Instead, I managed to make my voice as sweet as possible and keep the lie in motion. "I forgive you," I said once again.

I staggered into the bathroom. In a daze I grasped the edges of the sink and lifted my head to see in the mirror. What I saw scared me. The face wasn't mine. My black hair was sticking up all over the place. My eyes were blue-black and swollen almost completely shut. The blood vessels in my eyes had burst, and what little I could see of my eyeballs was all red. Blood trickled from my nose.

I put my finger against my mouth, expecting to only feel my gums. I was shocked to find my teeth still intact. I looked down at my shredded blouse and drew my hands up to my face. Ironically, the mirror reflected my perfectly manicured nails against a face I didn't recognize.

I managed to wipe some of the blood away from my nose, but it kept flowing. I tilted my head back and applied pressure to stop the bleeding as I'd been taught in nursing school. My head felt as if it would explode.

The telephone rang, and I could hear Fred's laughter drift down the hall to the bathroom. Demons mocked me as I eavesdropped. "Oh, Jackie and I are just sitting around doing nothing. We may come over later," he lied.

This man is crazy! my thoughts screamed. *I've got to get out of here!*

While he was still on the phone I grabbed his keys from the bedroom and made a beeline for his truck. Fred dropped the phone in mid-sentence and ran after me yelling, "You get back here!"

I knew I was as good as dead if he caught me, so I ran with all of my might, leaped into the front seat of the truck, and locked the doors. My hands shook as I fumbled to get the key into the ignition. Fred cursed and pulled at the door handle with all of his strength.

I turned to see his fist pulled back, aiming straight at the window. I floored the accelerator with the gear in reverse. The tires screeched, and the pickup lunged backward with Fred still holding on to the side like a wild man. I put the gear in forward and fishtailed across the field until I flung him loose from the truck.

In my rearview mirror I could see him punching the air with his fists, and I can only imagine what he was shouting. I left him behind in a cloud of dust.

My heart pounded, and I could barely see the road. I drove straight to the police station and stumbled into the entrance, trembling from head to toe. "Please, somebody help me!" I cried, before collapsing into a chair.

A police officer gently looked down at me. "Ma'am, can you tell me what happened?"

Through blood and tears I managed to piece together the terrifying incident, although no words could describe the terror I had experienced. Fred's beating was worse than all the beatings from my first marriage combined.

I later read in the police report that the two officers who were sent to make the arrest had to call for backup. Fred threatened them, and they were forced to break into the trailer. With his legs in shackles and his wrists in handcuffs, Fred was taken to jail.

I filed charges the same day. I'll never forget the look on his face when he saw me through the cell bars. Through gritted teeth he threatened, "I'll kill you. You'd better get a gun. I'll come and get you. You'll never be able to hide from me!"

Exposed Heart

His words haunted me night and day. I knew beyond a shadow of a doubt that he would make good on his promise. And I never found out what I had done to provoke such hatred.

Chapter Eight

Achy Breaky Heart

The blue light from the television screen cast an eerie glow across the room. I sensed the eyes of a stranger peering at me through the screen door. Somebody was watching me. I held my breath as I eased off my chair and tiptoed to the bedroom to get my gun. A minute later I heard the doorknob turn, and the door slowly began to open. Chills raced up and down my spine. I was no longer safe.

After my divorce from Fred I lived in constant fear. I bought a small gun to calm my nerves in case he came after me as he had threatened. Nightmares of him finding me left me shaking and crying through the night. I didn't know how much more my nerves could take.

When word got back to Chuck that Fred had beaten me, Chuck threatened to kill Fred. I learned this through a co-worker who had befriended Chuck when they had worked together years earlier. His need to protect and defend me was both amusing and frustrating. It was crazy. I thought to myself, *Now isn't that the pot calling the kettle black!*

The kids and I moved back to my parents' house, and I went to work at the ammunition plant where Chuck had worked right after we were married. My job as an assembly line worker gave me some extra money to pay for the children's school clothes and visits to the doctor and dentist. It was not an exciting job by any means. I inspected hand grenades, which traveled slowly by on a conveyer belt. While I hated the idea of Americans fighting in Vietnam, I was thankful to have a job.

The blast should never have happened. It was a stupid mistake made by a co-worker who had accidentally pulled the pin out of a live grenade. He lost his arm as he tried to toss the exploding grenade behind a barricade built to shield us from this sort of thing

The enormous blast knocked me off my chair and onto the floor. Debris fell all around me. One worker lost his eye. I thought I had escaped injury until someone said, "Jackie, you've got blood coming out of your ears." I put my hand to my ear and felt the warm liquid draining onto the palm of my hand.

Within minutes ambulances arrived at the plant. All the wounded were taken to the hospital. I remember lying on a gurney as hospital staff ran in every direction. Doctors barked orders. Nurses tried to calm frantic patients. The shrill of ambulance sirens echoed in the background. We were thousands of miles from Vietnam, but we'd gotten a glimpse of what one grenade could do.

The doctor who examined my ears told me one eardrum had burst during the explosion, which explained why my ears were filled with a high-pitched ringing sound and why I suffered from deafness in my left ear. The nerves in my ears were significantly damaged, which disrupted my equilibrium. As a result, I could no longer drive without getting dizzy. I could barely stand up without becoming nauseated.

The explosion resurrected memories of a serious injury I had suffered when I was four years old. I had been playing on a clothesline when my hands slipped and I fell several feet to the ground. The fall knocked the breath out of me, and I was unable to move. My parents were afraid that I was paralyzed.

Slowly, I regained movement in my arms and legs, but my back never stopped aching. As the years passed, my back continued to hurt. The fear that I would be deaf or unable to walk or drive jolted me back to that experience I'd had as a child.

The constant ringing in my ear was also taking a toll on my nerves. I received a series of B-12 shots for my balance and was told I would have to continue taking them for the rest of my life. I was given a leave of absence from my job until my injury healed.

Each day I grew more and more dependent on tranquilizers and anxiety pills. I looked forward to the calming effect they had on my body. As the days, weeks, and months crept by, I became more dependent on the medication to get me through the day. My senses stayed numb, and I lived life on an even keel. Nothing bothered me. The pills bandaged my emotional pain and allowed me to escape reality.

A year after my injury I decided it was time to get back on my feet, to make something of my life, and to quit depending on my parents for food and shelter. I did some soul-searching and concluded that my best shot was to become a licensed beautician. For as long as I could remember, I had loved to style hair. It made perfect sense.

Avery didn't have anything that resembled a beauty school, so I enrolled in cosmetology school in Paris, Texas. I'd get up in the morning to make the fifty-mile drive, but the medication made me so groggy that most days I stopped on the side of the road to sleep it off. Being late for school frustrated me. I'd leave the house at nine in the morning and pull into the school around noon, when the trip should have taken no more than an hour.

After several weeks of getting to school late, I was introduced to a drug that promised to offset the drowsy effects of the medication. They were called black mollies, and they promised to give me energy to get through the day. And they did. I could pop one pill in the morning and have enough energy for myself and seven other people.

This became my routine—uppers in the morning, downers at night. I hated the feeling of depression that followed after the high wore off, but it was the only way I could function. The ups and downs became a way of survival.

My social life began to pick up after months of sitting at home. I did the nightclub scene even while I was living with my parents. It was a way to further escape my pain. Besides, as hard as I tried, I could not make the yearning for a husband go away. I daydreamed about getting married. The impulse to tie the knot once again grew from an innocent thought to an obsessive drive.

I had put a hundred faces in my "happily ever after" picture, but whenever a flaw surfaced in a man I was dating or engaged to, I'd break off the relationship. I toyed with many a heart. My mother once told me, "If you get engaged one more time, I don't want to hear about it!"

A part of me still wanted to live the dream of being married, but the men I attracted were nothing like the man I wanted to marry. They were nothing like my father. I'd step into a relationship just enough to get my feet wet and to get a ring on my finger, and then I'd sabotage the whole thing by initiating a fight.

After two years of doing the nightclub scene, a friend introduced me to a country-western singer named Mike. He was the road manager and opening act for singer Ray Price. My heart fluttered whenever I heard Mike sing. He recorded a great song by Kris Kristofferson, "I Love Her, Good or Bad, She's Mine." When the lights went down and he began to sing a love ballad, I pretended he was singing the songs just for me.

I had nothing to lose the day a friend asked me if I wanted to meet Mike. His qualifications sounded like characteristics from my "ideal man" list: singer and songwriter, passionate, nice-looking, and tall, with a boyish charm that melted my heart.

Mike and I hit it off from the start. Everything about him appealed to my craving for adventure, romance, and security. His future as a country-western singer looked bright. And I could only imagine how wonderful it would be hearing him strum his guitar and serenade me with love songs.

Even the nasty details of his recent divorce weren't enough to deter me from pursuing the relationship. So what if the divorce had left a hole in his heart? I could be the one to fill the hole left by his ex-wife, nicknamed Boots. And as for his three sons, well, I'd eventually win their hearts, and we would be one happy, blended family.

The first part of my plan worked, and we married after dating only five months. Unfortunately, I never stopped hearing about "Boots and the boys," as he affectionately referred to them. It sounded like the title of a country-western song to me. I tried not to let his fond memories of them threaten our relationship. But the way he talked on and on about his boys and his ex-wife secretly worried me.

I pushed my fears aside and faithfully attended the concerts as the proud wife of the opening act. Ray Price's wife, Janie, was about my age, and we quickly became friends. We sat together at concerts. It was like living in a fantasy world every night, with all the bright lights, dazzling rhinestones, huge crowds—and money. It was a lifestyle I knew I could adjust to well.

Janie became the friend I had always dreamed of having. She was the type of person I could count on to be there when I needed someone to talk to. She was someone I could depend on.

Once when Mikey fell and chipped his two front teeth, Janie took him to the dentist and paid the bill. She was always buying groceries for us. She blessed me as no friend had ever done before.

I felt like the luckiest woman in the world, and I was happy with Mike. He never abused me with his words or his fist. He treated me with gentleness and kindness. But I knew I didn't have his heart, even though he told me he loved me. "Boots and the boys" were always on his mind. I often wondered if he was singing about his ex-wife when he strummed his guitar in the moonlight, singing songs of lost loves and broken hearts.

I loved Mike and gave him all of me. He, in turn, acted as if he loved me, too. He was a calm and gentle soul. We purchased a new house in a small town outside Dallas. The land had been cleared for our house, and the day we moved in there were no trees, bushes, lawn, or fence—nothing but dirt and a house. I hung newspaper over the windows until we could afford draperies. I loved the smell of the new cabinets and freshly painted walls as well as the cleanliness of my new home. It was a new beginning for my children and me.

Once you've been beaten to a pulp, you tend to fear certain types of men. But I had no reason to fear for my physical safety in my own house—until one night when Mike was out of town doing a show.

I was watching television because I was having a hard time getting to sleep. Mikey and Charlsey were asleep in their beds.

The back porch light was on. Suddenly, I felt as if someone was watching me. I glanced toward the patio door and could see an eye peering through a little hole in our newspaper "curtain."

Casually, I switched off the television and walked into my bedroom where I kept my gun. The door began to rattle. I could see the doorknob turn. I walked back to the den and phoned the police, "Help! Please help me!" I begged in a panicked whisper. "Someone is trying to break in and kill me!"

I gave my address, and the operator told me to stay on the phone.

I heard the lock jiggle and the back door creak as it started to open. Instinctively, I did the only thing I knew to do to protect myself. I kept one ear to the telephone receiver, aimed the gun at the patio door, and pulled the trigger on that little .25 automatic.

The glass shattered, and I tried to get a good look at the intruder. I succeeded in getting a glimpse of a man, but not enough to recognize him. He was running, and I heard him scream out in pain. I knew I had shot him.

The police dispatcher said, "What...what happened? Are you OK?"

"I think I just killed somebody," I answered in a quivering voice.

The police arrived shortly after my call. A detective walked all around the house and spotted footprints at every window. Obviously the stranger had peered in the windows before attempting a break-in. The prowler was more than a Peeping Tom; he could be dangerous. When I saw the muddy footprints, I knew immediately who my stalker was.

On one occasion, while our builder was going over some things with us regarding our new home, I noticed a hole in the bottom of his left shoe. There it was, imprinted in the mud—the perfect imprint of that hole.

I told the police. My suspicions were confirmed as I spotted small peepholes torn in the newspaper taped to the windows. It had to be our builder, who lived nearby. He was the only person outside the family that had been inside the house and could have torn holes in the newspaper. He was a very sick man—who may have had more on his mind that night than watching me undress for bed—who had planned everything in advance.

The police went to the man's house to question him that night. His wife answered the door and told the officers he'd been home all evening. The police told her about the shoe imprint. The man appeared at his door with dirt caked on his shoes and a fresh scrape beneath his left eye, where either flying glass or a bullet had passed very close.

The only evidence they had was circumstantial, since I didn't get a look at his face and his wife provided an alibis for his whereabouts during the time of the break-in attempt. There was not enough evidence to make an arrest. As I thought about it, I was certain he'd had keys made to all the doors. There was no doubt in my mind who the perpetrator was!

I called Mike's brother, and he and his wife came over and sat up with me all that night, consoling me. Night after night I was haunted by the break-in, and I didn't feel safe, especially with Mike out of town. To make matters worse I began to receive "heavy breathing" calls when Mike was away. I knew who it was.

My sense of security was destroyed. I continued to carry a gun in my pocket wherever I went. I became paranoid. I'd sprinkle baby powder in front of all the doors when I'd leave the house in the morning for beauty school. When I returned home I would shove open the door to look for footprints before setting foot in my house. I lived in constant fear.

Our marriage survived a year of Mike's traveling and the attempted break-in, but the one thing it couldn't survive was Mike's affection for "Boots and the boys." He couldn't stop talking about them. Sometimes when we were together he'd be a million miles away, even though he was right beside me. Now the shoe was on the other foot. I was married to someone who couldn't love me.

I loaded the car one morning to go to Austin, Texas, to take the state board test to get my cosmetology license. Before leaving I turned to Mike and said, "When I get back I don't want to hear anymore about 'Boots and the boys,' or it's over."

When I returned home, I discovered he had packed his bags and left. I guess you could say he honored my request, because I never heard about "Boots and the boys" again. Mike returned to the place his heart had never left. This time, *my* heart was broken in two.

Chapter Nine

God, Let Me Die!

Shadows danced across my bedroom wall as I lay awake. I prayed the same prayer over and over again each night: "God, please don't let me wake up. Please take my life while I sleep. I can't handle another day." God never answered, and I'd wake up more tired than when I went to bed. I was at the end of my rope...and it seemed like death was the only way out of my horrible life. I dug the razor's edge into my skin and wept silent tears as the blood ran down my arm.

The breakup of my third marriage devastated me. Once again, I was alone with two children to raise. My hopes and dreams were dashed by yet another failure. The attempted break-in had left me terrified of the dark and of being alone. It infuriated me that the builder had taken away my sense of security. I never felt safe again, even after I moved to an apartment far away from that terrible man.

I carried a gun wherever I went. I was more paranoid than ever. I always felt as if a stalker was following me. I expected someone to jump out from behind a door or from the shadows as I walked by. It seemed as if the only time I felt OK was when I was drinking or taking prescription medication. I hated being sober.

I spent more and more time in night-clubs and began smoking to calm my nerves.

I can't say that it happened overnight, but gradually I reached a point where I was going out almost every night to escape my fear and loneliness. My life became a vicious cycle of booze and men. Oh, I'd tell myself night after night, *This is it. This is the last time!*

But I couldn't stop.

During the day I'd fool myself into thinking that I was in control. In my mind I would plan the supper I was going to cook for my children, and picture myself reading their favorite bedtime story and tucking them in with a good-night kiss. But as I watched the sun go down, the tug-of-war battle would begin to rage inside me.

You've got to stop going to clubs!

What harm will it do to go one more time?

I argued with myself back and forth as I began the nightly ritual of getting ready for the inevitable. Panty hose. Tight dress. High heels. Nail polish. Perfume. Makeup. Hair spray. Baby-sitter. The seduction to go out was stronger than my willpower to stay home. The voice of my rebellion won out each and every night.

I was an addict.

I've heard about many forms of addiction. I've heard about gambling addiction, drug and alcohol addiction, food addiction, and sex addiction, but my addiction was something I'd never heard of before. I truly was addicted to the night-club scene. The routine of getting dressed up had an anesthetic effect on me. Sitting in the club, drinking, and dancing were all a part of the high. The entire night's experience was like a drug. Each night I told myself, *Jackie, this could be your lucky night. This could be the night you meet the man of your dreams.*

Some may argue that the impulse to go to night-clubs is a type of sex addiction. Maybe it is. I'm sure I paired up with sex addicts left and right, but for me sex didn't have to be a part of the experience. What compelled me to go out each night was my fear of missing Mr. Right rather than my need for sex.

I would drag myself home after the clubs closed and fall into bed, safe again with my babies. The letdown came the next morning. I hated myself. I woke up too tired and depressed to get out of bed. When I did manage to push back the covers and roll out of bed, one look in the mirror sent me back. I despised the woman who stared back at me. The dark circles under my bloodshot eyes mocked me. I was so young and yet so old. *I'm never going out again!* I promised myself.

The more I struggled to get free, the more ensnared I became. Every time I tried to quit, I'd go right back, more drawn to the night-clubs than ever. I was addicted to this lifestyle and hated myself for it.

God does give us warning signs along life's journey: *Watch out! Stop! Go back!* In His sovereignty He makes a way of escape for us each time sin crouches at our heart's door. Had I listened to God's warnings I would have been spared much sorrow, but I had stopped listening to the voice of the Holy Spirit long before. Thankfully, He was not finished speaking to me.

Exposed Heart

During the summer of 1972 God managed to get my attention. I was on my way to work at a local beauty shop. For the first time in my life I had finished what I had started out to do. I had passed the cosmetology exam and was now a licensed beautician. I was proud of my career.

One day as I was stopped at a red light, I glanced in my rearview mirror and watched in horror as a car came speeding up behind me with no indication that it would be stopping any time soon.

Whammm!

The impact threw me against the steering wheel and onto the floorboard. I wasn't wearing a seat belt. In my vanity, all I could think about was the hairpiece that was now off my head and nowhere to be found. Earlier that morning I had used at least twenty bobby pins to secure my wig in place, because my greatest fear was having a gust of wind blow it right off my head. I suppose I was in shock, because I didn't think about the fact that I may have been injured. I was worried about the way I looked!

A man in the car in front of me was the first person to check on me. He was unable to open the door, so he yelled through the window, "Lady, are you all right? I thought your head came off when your hairpiece snapped off and fell in the backseat. I'm glad to see that you weren't beheaded!"

On impact, my body had jerked forward and back, and the force had snapped my wig right off my head! I managed to grab it and put it back on by the time the wrecking crew got there to pry open the door and get me out. I don't know how the workers kept from laughing. When I caught sight of my reflection, I realized my hairpiece was on sideways!

My looks were so important to me. I felt as if that was all I had going for me. The wig incident was a blow to my vanity, and I sometimes wonder if God allowed that to happen just to remind me that He cares more about the condition of my heart and my relationship with Him than He does about my appearance.

Not only was my ego deflated but also the wreck totaled Janie's new Cadillac. To make matters worse, the doctors told me that the impact had ruptured a disc in my back and I would need to undergo surgery.

Suddenly, my life was on hold, and I had a lot of time to think.

Recovery from the surgery forced me to stay in bed for several weeks. No night-clubs. No friends. Just day after day filled with time to examine my life and where I was heading. My family came to the rescue with meals, child care, and love, but I was unable to fully appreciate their attempts to express God's love and kindness until years later.

God had called "time-out!" to deliver me from an addictive lifestyle. It was a perfect opportunity for me to escape from that chaotic existence by breaking free of the cycle of addiction. But I missed the chance and allowed self-pity to consume me. All I could think about was how unfair life had been to me. Gradually, I slipped into a depression.

Those days and weeks were some of the loneliest times of my life, because my addiction could no longer satisfy the emptiness inside my soul. It was as if a part of my heart had been chiseled away, leaving a vacuum. For the first time I felt despair over the wrong choices I had made in my life. Even the pain medication couldn't numb the emptiness I was feeling in my soul.

After the accident I began taking an increased dosage of pain medication and muscle relaxers. I couldn't function without drugs in my system. I needed drugs to get out of bed. I needed drugs to make it through the day. I needed drugs to go to sleep. I know that my reasoning was skewed, because I took pleasure in being on so much medication. It validated that I was a victim. I didn't have to take responsibility for my condition; it was not my fault.

Within a few months I was back to my old ways, going to night-clubs every night I could. I had quit my job after the accident; during the day—when I wasn't sleeping—I would try to figure out a way to put food on the table. My meager savings wasn't enough to cover the increasing medical bills, let alone meet our basic need for rent, clothing, and food.

Welfare seemed to be the only answer, because I was too ashamed to ask my family for help. We barely had enough to eat at times, so I swallowed my pride and applied for government assistance. I remember dressing up just to go cash my government checks, knowing full well that people probably thought I was taking advantage of the system, because I didn't look poor. But I didn't want to be a hypocrite and dress down to satisfy other people. I dressed up for everything else I did, so why should this be any different?

The welfare checks helped us out with food and doctor fees, but other bills were coming in faster than I could pay them. I couldn't support my lifestyle. It was like going from anthill-sized debt to a mountain of debt. I didn't see any way out. The situation was hopeless.

I had no job. I believed that I was stupid. I only saw myself as a failure. I believed the only thing I had going for me was my looks. The only time I felt I had any value was when a man would say I was pretty. But not even looks could get me out of the financial bondage I was in.

Prostitution is a taboo subject in certain segments of our society. Many people simply don't want to face the fact that every day, young women and men sell their bodies for drugs and money—or that many prostitutes are not the stereotypical streetwalker but rather ordinary people who are trapped into thinking that they have no other hope. They've reached the end of their resources, and in desperation they look to the only thing they have worth selling—their bodies. And they know there's always a buyer out there somewhere. Of course, it's the devil who set the trap in the first place and then deceived them into thinking there's no other choice. But it's all a lie.

Yes, for a time I did consider this to be a viable option for me. Thankfully, before I could act on it, my family saw my need and rallied to support me. But my desperate situation opened my eyes to how easily a person could be lured into Satan's snare. If I hadn't had my family, I believe I could have easily fallen into a dangerous lifestyle of increasing bondage, one that in too many cases ends even in death.

The accident was the catalyst God used to make me see what I had become. But instead of seeking His mercy, I pleaded with Him, "Please, just take my life while I sleep. I don't want to wake up. God, let me die!"

When God didn't answer my prayer, I began to "practice" committing suicide. I would press the razor's edge into my arm. The slight sting of the blade against my flesh made me feel in control. I knew with a little added pressure, I would hold a life-and-death decision in my hands. Slowly, as the attempts became more frequent and more serious, I realized just how out of control I was.

I continued to pray my death wish each night, to no avail. I'd wake up the next morning with sunshine invading my bedroom and realize I still had a pulse. And as hard as I tried, I couldn't shut out the still, small voice of the Holy Spirit speaking to me; His mercies really are new every morning.

All along God wanted me to experience death. I don't mean a physical death; He wanted me to lay down all my hopes, dreams, and expectations at the cross. He wanted me to place all of my addictions, fears, and failures at His feet. He wanted all of me, so He could make me a vessel of His mercy, love, and grace.

A part of me really did want to die. But something kept me going. I tend to think it was two parents who cried out to God on my behalf. My sins were no longer hidden from them; they knew full well that I was as far away from the Lord as I'd ever been. Backslidden, they called it.

There was no doubt that somebody, somewhere was praying for me.

Chapter Ten

Over the Edge

The metal door slammed behind me, and the turn of the lock was a stark reminder that I was no longer a free woman. The cold emptiness of the holding cell mirrored the reality of my lonely, miserable life. As the hours crept by, I paced the cell like a caged animal. A hundred questions darted in and out of my brain. What would happen to Charlsey and Mikey? Who would raise my new baby? What if Sonny died and I was convicted of murder? What if I spent the rest of my life in prison? What if I never got to hold my children again? Demons taunted me as I faced the possibility of losing everything I loved.

The aroma of popcorn, mingled with blood-curdling screams, filled the amusement park as I ushered my children down the ramp that led to the double-looped roller coaster. Charlsey, nine, and Mike, eleven, climbed on and braced themselves for a few minutes of fear and fun. I shouted my last-second motherly warnings: "Don't stick your arms out!" and "Hold on!" I waved and tried to focus on the two small figures that whizzed by me in a blur of bright color.

My life was like the roller coaster. Many times I wanted to scream, *Stop! I can't handle it anymore! I want to get off!* But my life kept moving faster and faster, the turns and twists becoming sharper and more painful.

Until this point in my life, I had never considered the possibility that someone would try to harm my children. I had always been the one who bore the brunt of a man's drunken rage.

My children were innocent. There was no reason for any man to harm them or take advantage of them. My eyes were opened to the evil that can be in a person's soul the day Charlsey began behaving strangely. Her bubbly personality had vanished.

I asked her what was wrong.

I sat in disbelief as she told me how my boyfriend had pulled down his pants in front of her. He told Charlsey things that robbed her of her innocent mind.

The rage I felt was something too powerful to describe. It was the first time that I knew I was capable of killing someone. I hated this man with every bone in my body. If he had been anywhere in sight as Charlsey anguished over what she had seen and heard, I know I would have killed him.

My trust of men took a nosedive after that episode. I came to the conclusion that men couldn't be trusted. Period. I knew now that if they didn't hurt me, they would hurt my child. I swore that I would never bring a man around my children again.

The episode with Charlsey wasn't enough, however, to divert me from the night-club scene. My addiction had taken control of my life. Not even my distrust of men could keep me from looking for the perfect man, somebody like my father. I kept putting on those rose-colored glasses.

The next man I dated was a wealthy Italian named Tony. He threw money around as if he owned Dallas, and although I didn't care for him that much, he kept buying me things that made me happy. He basically bought my affection with gifts.

Tony treated me like a queen, but at the same time he started to act as if he owned me. His possessiveness began to drive me away, and I started going to clubs alone or with my girlfriends.

One night I had just ordered my first drink when a tall, handsome man I'd never seen before strutted over to my table. "Will you dance with me?" he asked with an air of confidence.

I swirled the drink in my glass and tried to avoid his eyes. I felt shy. I always did before the drink kicked in. "No, thank you," I answered.

A few minutes later another man walked up to me and said, "I can't believe you turned my friend down. You see him sitting over there?" he asked, pointing to a man in a tailored jacket. "Well, his name is Sonny, and he's got more money than you can imagine! There are women who'd give anything for his attention!"

I looked in the direction of his pointing finger. Sonny lifted his drink to me and flashed a contagious smile. I smiled back. Now it was a game. "No, thanks," I said again.

Sonny kept sending his friends over to ask me to dance. I ignored his cockiness and admired his persistence. After a couple of drinks I was more easily persuaded.

We danced until the club closed.

I suppose it was a combination of factors that attracted me to Sonny. Handsome features, a big car, an entourage of men with bulging muscles that Sonny proudly claimed to be bodyguards, the wad of money, his generosity. It was no secret that he was involved in shady deals, but he treated me with more respect than I'd ever been shown before, and I was a sucker for his take-charge personality.

Well, Tony didn't take too kindly to the fact that he'd lost his woman to a high-rolling businessman. He confronted Sonny one night in the parking lot outside my apartment building. I was inside with my children when gunfire erupted. I pushed my children to the floor and screamed for them to stay down.

The shooting finally stopped. I peeked through the window to see Tony getting into his car and watched him drive away. Sonny and his bodyguards were unharmed. They stuffed their handguns back into hidden places. Miraculously, no one was hurt.

I never heard from Tony again.

In the spring of 1973 it was time to do it again. Like clockwork, I had married two years after each divorce. That made it four husbands in eleven years.

Sonny and I were married in a small ceremony in Laredo, Mexico, conducted by a justice of the peace whose heavy Mexican accent made it next to impossible to understand a word he was saying. We both said "I do" and were given a certificate that sealed our marriage vows.

We spent our honeymoon in a run-down Mexican hotel. The room was stuffy. There was no air-conditioning. We opened the windows hoping for a slight breeze. Instead, our room invited flies to buzz in and out all day.

I was disgusted. My thoughts screamed, *What am I doing in a crummy hotel? It wasn't supposed to be like this! I'm married to a rich, powerful man, and this is the best he can do?*

The memories of the pain and frustration of my past honeymoons came one after another, making me relive each horrible, disappointing moment. And there was nothing I could do about it. I left Mexico wondering if all men were alike, charming and loving and generous until they exchanged vows with me.

But I knew they were not all alike. I had a father who treated my mother with respect and gentleness. He would have given her the moon and the stars on a silver platter if he could have. He always gave my mother the best he could offer, even if it was simple by the world's standards. Why couldn't I find a man like him?

The fighting erupted soon after the honeymoon. Sonny came stumbling into the bedroom in the early hours of the morning with the heavy scent of perfume and stale smoke clinging to his jacket. I demanded that he tell me what he'd been doing. He answered with a slap across my face. The burning sensation and the imprint of his hand on my cheek became a constant reminder that I was supposed to keep my mouth shut. Night after night, Sonny made it clear that he had no intention of settling down.

I never considered leaving him, because I truly loved Sonny. And I was convinced that he loved me. He just had an unusual way of showing it. He bought me nice things like furs and expensive jewelry. We bought a lovely home in a suburban neighborhood in Arlington, Texas, and I filled it with beautiful furniture, china, draperies, and antiques, along with a brand-new Cadillac for the garage.

Exposed Heart

I was the beautiful, well-dressed wife of a big-time businessman. My job was to make Sonny look good. Sonny convinced me that I was stupid and even said so in front of his friends. I had no chance of making it on my own. I needed him. He needed me. It was like some sick business deal, except for the fact that I loved him.

I found out that I was pregnant after we had been married only four months. I knew right away that this was not good news. Sonny was adamant about the fact that he didn't want any more children. His ex-wife was raising his two small children, while I was raising my two. That was enough for Sonny. But nevertheless I was pregnant. Charlsey and Mike went on and on about the baby. They'd take turns pressing their hands against my watermelon-sized belly until they detected a thump or kick. Then they would giggle with delight until the next movement.

Their excitement slowly began to rub off on me. In spite of all the emotional pain and all the mistakes, I began to see this unborn child as a new beginning for me. I vowed that I would never go back to the night-club scene. I would be a content, married woman who spent the day wiping runny noses, kissing boo-boos, and saying good-night prayers.

The day our son Howard was born, God smiled on me. Howard was so alert, and he had the most beautiful dimples. The greatest gift was when Sonny held his new baby for the first time. I watched, misty-eyed, as every inch of that powerful man melted when he looked into his son's eyes. He was a proud daddy, and there was no hiding it.

At that moment it seemed as if all the mistakes I'd made, all the wrong choices, all the abuse, dissolved into a sea of overwhelming joy. My life was finally going to amount to something. I may have failed at everything else, but my new son gave me a purpose for living.

I gathered Charlsey, now ten years old, and Mikey, twelve, to my side as we shared the happiness of that moment. Their eyes danced with excitement as they watched their newborn brother cradled in my arms. Our little family had grown. We were a team, and nothing, absolutely nothing, could tear us apart.

Howard was one week old when we got an unexpected call from Sonny's ex-wife asking if we would raise his two children—little Sonny, who was five years old, and Ann, who was three. She rambled on about her battle with alcoholism and depression and how she needed time away from the stress of motherhood. I was sympathetic, but when Sonny told her yes, I hit the roof!

"How in the world do you expect me to raise five children? I'm just learning how to handle three!" I yelled. "You can't be serious!"

Sonny had an iron will, and once his mind was made up nothing could change it. It was an open-and-shut case. These were his children, his call, and yet I would be the one to raise them. He could come and go as he pleased and pocket the money he had been shelling out for child support, and I couldn't do a thing about it! My perfect world collapsed in one day.

There I was, at twenty-eight years old, raising a twelve-year-old, a ten-year-old, and a newborn—plus two stepchildren, ages five and three. Little Sonny and Ann didn't care for their new arrangement any more than I did. They begged and cried to go home to their mother.

I didn't blame them.

Nights were hard for everyone, because that's when little Sonny and Ann missed their own beds and wanted their mommy to give them a good-night kiss.

Howard was a healthy baby whose strong lungs reminded me when he needed to be changed and fed, and as with any newborn, he alerted me to his needs throughout the night. Charlsey and Mike learned to sleep through most of the cries and screams, but I never could. It was a nightmare that Sonny didn't have to endure. He stayed away most of the time. I was convinced that God had played a cruel joke on me.

The afternoon started out like any other. I hadn't slept a wink the previous night. Sonny casually walked into the bedroom after being gone all night and began to change his clothes. I was filled with rage and jealousy. I knew Sonny had spent the night with another woman, but I couldn't prove it. My instincts, though, told me I was right.

While Sonny took a shower, I rummaged through his pockets until I found what I was hoping not to find. I pulled out a book of matches from A Place Across the Street—the same bar where we had met three years earlier. I opened the flap and found the name of a woman and a phone number scribbled on the inside cover in Sonny's handwriting. Jealousy consumed me, and the anger inside me erupted.

"Where have you been all night? Who were you with? How long have you been seeing this woman?" I screamed, shaking the book of matches in his face.

He scowled, "I'm fed up with you! I'm leaving!"

By the look in his eyes and the tone in his voice, I knew Sonny meant it. The thought of being left alone with five small children, trapped inside a world out of my control, was too much for me to take.

I snapped.

He headed into the kitchen as I went to find my gun. He had a blank look on his face as he watched me aim at the china cabinet and fire. Glass shattered. I fired again and hit a china plate. It broke into tiny pieces. "You broke the dish!" he raged.

For a moment, I thought, *He's going to beat me up if I don't kill him. I'll pay for this!* I braced myself for an attack. Sonny didn't even bother to look at me. He turned to walk out the door. This enraged me more.

I aimed the gun at Sonny and pulled the trigger a third time. He walked a few steps across the room and collapsed onto the floor. His face grew white and pale. Blood spilled out of his body onto the floor.

I felt crazy. Cruel. Mean. I wanted to see him suffer. I wanted him to die.

I walked to his side, and I held that little gun to the side of his head. "Did you dance with her?" I asked.

I needed to know. I needed to hear that he had not been unfaithful to me, even though I knew it was a lie.

He shook his head no.

If he had said yes, I would have pulled the trigger a fourth time.

While sitting beside my unmoving husband, my thoughts raced. *What would I do if he was faking? What if he suddenly jumped up and beat the tar out of me?* I could see it in my mind. He would spring up and beat me to within an inch of my life.

I stood. My hands trembled as I aimed the gun at Sonny's head. His face was growing more and more pale. Reality bit me. *Oh, my God, he's dying!* my thoughts screamed.

I grabbed the phone and called a deputy sheriff who was a friend of Sonny's. "I shot Sonny! I shot him!" I screamed into the receiver.

"Have you called an ambulance?" he asked.

"No!" I cried.

"Jackie, hang up and call an ambulance immediately. I'm on my way."

The police and ambulance pulled up at the same time. As they loaded Sonny onto the stretcher, he managed to say in a weak voice, "It was an accident." His voice trailed off as they cupped the oxygen mask over his nose and mouth.

I hated him for trying to defend me. I hated him more than I'd ever hated anyone. "No, I meant to do it! I meant to shoot him! I wanted him dead! I can't take it anymore!" I yelled, as an officer clasped handcuffs over my wrists.

The officer placed me in the back of the patrol car and took me to jail. They fingerprinted me and took my picture. I now had a permanent record.

The ride was finally over.

Chapter Eleven

Worldly Riches

Like the ebb and flow of the ocean tides, my emotions drifted back and forth, in and out, from wanting God to wanting all the dazzle the world offered. I was a high-society girl now, pleased to finally obtain the attention and worldly riches I had so desired from the time I was a child. The glitz and glamour swept me off my feet. Then, unexpectedly, the move of God's spirit became a current too strong to ignore.

I had been in jail for the better part of a day when I heard footsteps and the jangling of keys outside my holding cell. The guard unlocked the door and delivered the news. "You're free to go home. It looks like your husband isn't going to press charges," he said nonchalantly.

His words hung in the air until I grasped their meaning. I leaned against the barren wall, hardly believing what he had just said. The tears I tried so hard to stifle came spilling freely down my face. I'd just been given a second chance.

I followed the officer to the main desk and signed a few papers. My hand trembled as I pulled open the door and breathed deep breaths of fresh autumn air. I was finally going home.

My heart pounded as I imagined myself holding my newborn son against my breast once again, something I vowed I would never take for granted. Imagining his tiny fingers curled around mine made my heart leap. I'm free! my heart cried.

After making sure my children were taken care of, I drove to the hospital to see Sonny. I walked into his room and leaned over him. My conscience was numb. I didn't feel guilt. As a matter of fact, I didn't feel much of anything except for a slight upset stomach as I fought back the odor of the sterile hospital, a smell I had learned to hate back in my nursing school days.

"So what is his condition?" I asked the physician in charge.

The doctor rubbed his chin. I wondered if he knew I was the one who had done this horrible thing. If he did, he hid it well. I raised my eyebrows in anticipation of his report.

"In the medical world it's a good-news, bad-news situation," he said slowly. Too slowly. "The good news is that the position of the bullet is not life-threatening. Of course, if it had been one inch closer to his spine, it would have injured his spinal cord, perhaps paralyzing him from the waist down."

"And the bad news?" I asked.

After an almost unbearably long pause the doctor continued. "The bad news is that the bullet lodged in a place where any attempt to remove it would put Sonny at too great a risk," he replied. "In other words, he'll have to live with the bullet for the rest of his life."

While I was relieved that he had survived the shooting, in a twisted sort of way I was amused that Sonny would live the rest of his life with a little souvenir, a little reminder, of a woman's revenge. I was tired of being treated like a dog and being sent to my room while he and his friends took over the house whenever they pleased. I was the one who cleaned out the ashtrays, swept the floor, washed the glasses, and disposed of the empty whisky bottles after a night of drinking and gambling. I was the one who washed Sonny's clothes, making sure the lipstick prints didn't leave a stain.

I've often tried to piece together how a man like Sonny could change from a charming lover into an abusive husband who thought he had the right to treat me the way he did. It had started with a slap across the face. Who knows exactly when things changed. But gradually the slaps stung more and left the imprint of his hand across my cheek. Before I knew it, I was being kicked, beaten, and thrown against the wall, totally at the mercy of a man twice my size.

It's crazy. And yet, I always accepted the abuse as my lot in life. Somehow it had to be my fault. If I could just cook better, if I could only be more attractive, if I could keep my mouth shut and not argue back; if I wasn't so stupid, maybe, just maybe, the abuse would stop.

I leaned over the hospital bed and gently ran my fingers through his hair. I was in a daze. I was on automatic pilot, going through the motions, as if the shooting had never happened. "It's me, Jackie. Are you feeling all right?" I asked, sympathetically.

An agonizing moan escaped his pale lips.

"The doctor says you're going to be OK," I whispered.

Our eyes locked. And then, as soon as he noticed me, he drifted back to sleep. I drove home feeling rejected because Sonny didn't respond to my attempts to alleviate some of his anguish. How dare he ignore me. I'm his wife. I stood by this man's side through hell and high water, and this is how he repays me?

The full reality of what I had done hit me the moment I stepped into the dining room. A wave of nausea overwhelmed me. The shattered china plates and the bloodstains on the floor were a grisly reminder of the night before. I dropped to my knees and began to wail like a wounded animal. The sobs turned into a prayer: "Oh, God please have mercy on me and my marriage. I'm so sorry for what I did. I don't want to lose Sonny."

Sonny came home from the hospital a few days later. He would be confined to a wheelchair until the wound healed and his strength returned. I liked the fact that Sonny needed me more than he needed his friends. I dressed him, bathed him, and helped him to get in and out of bed. My roles were skewed, because I was both the wounder and healer.

I knew without a doubt that our marriage was heading straight toward a cliff. God was the only hope to save our rocky relationship. If God didn't change Sonny once and for all, I knew it was over. I pleaded with Him, "I beg You to change Sonny. Make him the right kind of husband to me and father to the kids. Please God...please!"

In spite of my prayer, a few nights later the same batch of unruly friends invaded my home, and to my disappointment, loaded Sonny and his wheelchair into a van. Once again, he was out on the town with his friends. A bullet in the back and all the praying in the world didn't stop Sonny from going back to his lifestyle.

He was the same. And I was the fool.

I found solace in the fact that the partying would take place away from our house. His pathetic friends were now afraid of me. I overheard one friend warn his pal, "Don't go in that house! Sonny's crazy wife might shoot you!"

The late-night drinking and gambling went on for years, but I could endure it since he no longer did these things in my presence. I was never again sent to my room like a disobedient child. That tiny morsel of respect made the marriage tolerable.

The screaming and fighting continued, but the physical abuse came and went like the passing seasons. I kept believing that someday it would stop.

But it never did.

Not long after the shooting we moved to another house. I was glad to leave the horrible memories that haunted me in my dreams. I hoped the move would erase the visions of Sonny's ashen face, the broken glass, and the blood.

The move was like a fresh start for us, and I wanted a new look to go along with the changes in my life. I stared into the mirror. My long black hair reminded me of the out-of-control me. Looking at pictures from that time I can see why people said I looked like Priscilla Presley did when she was married to Elvis, with her jet-black hair piled high and heavily made-up eyes.

I drove to the drugstore and bought a bottle of blond dye. Well, it didn't turn out anything like the color on the box. It turned my hair reddish-orange! When Sonny saw it he cried, "You look horrid!"

After several tries my hair turned blond, which was, in fact, very close to my natural color. Sonny turned up his nose once again, and said, "Some women look natural as a blond, but you're not one of them!"

That became a private joke between me and myself. Even though blond was my natural color, Sonny had only seen me with black hair. What could be more natural than the hair color a person is born with? His comment amused more than angered me.

Minutes turned into hours, hours into days, days into months. The new home and my new look didn't take away the unhappiness and loneliness that gnawed in the pit of my stomach. Day in and day out my hopes began to diminish, like melting snow revealing a muddy past with all its mistakes and regrets. Sonny would never change.

I stayed home most of the time. I had no friends. Little Sonny slowly began to respond to discipline, but Ann became more headstrong and resentful because she could not be with her mother. There were many days that the stress of meeting the individual needs of five children overwhelmed me, and I would bury my face in my pillow and cry.

For twelve years I raised Sonny's children. But no matter how hard I tried, I couldn't make Ann conform to being my little girl. To make matters worse, for those twelve years, their mother would call every few months to say, "Mind Jackie, because Mommy is sick and I can't take care of you. I'm still your mother, but Jackie is baby-sitting you, and you have to mind her."

I had accepted the children as mine, and I wanted them to be mine. I had invested many years into their lives. I resented their mother calling me the baby-sitter. She occasionally came to see them. But her phone calls were enough to upset them for weeks.

Eventually, little Sonny became like my own son. I grew to love him with all my heart. I loved Ann, too, but she had a hard time accepting me, and in a way, I don't blame her. She and little Sonny were uprooted overnight from their mother and placed in a new family. They had no say in the matter.

I've asked God to forgive me for the times I yelled at them and said hurtful things to them out of my own frustration and anger. They didn't deserve the life they had. The truth is that all my children had chaotic lives. The anger and abuse they witnessed for all those years makes me cringe. Their innocent eyes and ears should have never been exposed to those things.

In 1980 my life began to turn around. On the one hand I wanted to please God, and on the other hand, I wanted to please my husband. I was torn between two worlds. Sonny was making plenty of money, which allowed us to attend posh parties and socialize with Dallas' elite. We were friends with several of the Dallas Cowboys football players and their wives. We would routinely go to football games and parties afterward.

While the entertainment provided a temporary bandage for my pain, the next morning I'd wake up to the same feelings of loneliness and despair. All the razzle and dazzle the world offered me was not enough to fill the void in my heart. God was drawing me to back to Himself.

Chapter Twelve

No Turning Back

The road appeared to be little more than a blur as seen through my watery eyes. My knuckles were white as I clutched the steering wheel. Slowly, I pulled the car off to the side of the road and buried my face in my hands. The engine hummed idly as a groan too deep for words erupted from the depths of my soul. Years of suppressed shame and fear were pushed to the surface of my heart. It was time to stop running from God.

It was more out of guilt than a desire for my children to find God that I began to send them to a nearby church called Friendship Baptist. The bus ministry faithfully picked them up every Sunday morning and brought them safely home.

Charlsey was thirteen years old at the time. She accepted Jesus as her Savior one Sunday at church and was soon baptized. She would talk nonstop about what she had learned about Jesus every Sunday. Mike, little Sonny, and Ann also loved going to church.

Their enthusiasm for God made me feel lousy. I was a cowardly Christian going out on Saturday nights and then sleeping in on Sundays while my children attended church. The guilt gnawed at the depths of my soul.

But there was a bright spot: My sister Barbara, whose first marriage had just failed, found some much-needed comfort and therapy by pouring herself into serving the Lord. At the time, of course, I labeled her a fanatic and wondered why on earth she didn't just get a man and a life. At the same time, I did respect her deep down and didn't want her to know the kind of life I was living. But I knew she was praying for me; I could feel it.

She loved children and was among the Sunday school bus drivers at the Baptist church she attended. One Sunday morning, she picked up Mikey in the bus and took him to her church. On the way home, they talked about the Lord, and Mikey told his Aunt Barbara that he wanted to be saved. She pulled the bus into the parking lot of a nearby Safeway (an appropriate place, given the name!) and led him to the Lord right there. Even though I wasn't there, in my mind I can clearly see my little curly-headed, blond, blue-eyed boy looking very intense as he asked Jesus to come into his heart.

One weekend I had been out bargain-shopping at garage sales when I spotted a cassette tape by a well-known evangelist. I bought it and slid it into my car's cassette player.

The Holy Spirit began to deal with my heart as I listened to the tape. I didn't make it home. I pulled the car off to the side of the road. Tears streamed from my eyes. My heart was totally exposed. I buried my face in my hands as I prayed a prayer of total surrender to my heavenly Father: "God, use me any way that You want. I will follow You even if it means losing everything."

And I meant every word.

It's difficult to describe what happened at that moment. I felt as if a heavy chain had been broken and a weight had been lifted off my tormented soul. Peace and serenity surrounded me like a soft, warm blanket. The last time I felt that way had been during those late-night revival meetings listening to Sister Saxton when I was a child. Her words echoed from the past and penetrated my heart once again with a message of faith, hope, and love. It was time to stop running from God.

The following Sunday I visited a Baptist church near my home. Day after day I'd driven by the church and seen the sign on the lawn: "Happy Hour at 10:45 a.m." This sign encouraged me to at least give it a chance. I just couldn't imagine people having more fun at church than at a local club. I made up my mind to take my children to church with me. I thought they would be excited to visit with me.

I was wrong to assume that they would have no problems adjusting to a new congregation. Both churches were part of the same denomination, and I thought the children would be thrilled to join a church that I had selected. But I had uprooted my children and separated them from the church and the people they had grown to love and respect.

Charlsey was angry at first. Looking back, I regret not being more sensitive to my children's needs. They had grown to love Pastor Wade and the people at Friendship. I will be forever indebted to the people there who prayed for my children, loved them, and taught them the Bible.

Sunday after Sunday my hunger to know God grew. Sonny went once or twice. It didn't bother him that we went, but he made a point to tell me that he didn't want me nagging him about going to church or reading the Bible to him.

I was disappointed that Sonny balked when I asked him to give it a try. My children, on the other hand, began to love their new church. In fact, that was where Howard, at five years old, accepted Jesus as his Savior. I'll never forget that Sunday morning; Howard began tugging at the pastor's coat, saying, "I wanna get saved! I wanna get saved!"

Pastor Jack said, "We'll talk about it when you're older."

Howard insisted, "No! I want to get saved now!"

And so he did.

The chasm between Sonny and I widened. I knew our marriage was unstable. I became obsessed with detecting the slightest trace of perfume on Sonny's shirts. I continued to comb through his secret hiding places in search of other women's phone numbers.

Finally, I prayed and asked God to deliver me from the excessive jealousy and anger I felt toward Sonny. God did what I asked almost instantly. The insatiable need to play detective day and night disappeared. Jealousy no longer fueled my emotions.

A year later I was driving down a road, and another sign caught my eye. "Evangel Temple: New Year's Eve Service." Something drew me to that service. I enjoyed the worship and sermon so much that I joined the church. My children were uprooted. Again.

They began to love their new church as much as I did.

I prayed for Sonny more diligently than I ever had before. I wanted my husband to be by my side as our family basked in the presence of God. Sonny wouldn't budge! He wasn't about to give his life to Jesus, and he became angry when I nagged him to become a Christian.

It wasn't long before my house became a second sanctuary. I wanted my home to mirror the deep love and commitment I had for God. Religious poems, calendars, and pictures covered the walls. One day Sonny ordered me to remove the wall hangings from our bedroom, because he felt as if he was going to bed with the Virgin Mary. His sarcastic comment hurt, but it didn't discourage me from praying for him.

The Bible says that a woman can win her husband over with her pure behavior and her quiet spirit. I took this scripture to mean that I was to hold my tongue during his flare-ups, but it certainly wasn't easy. I always did have a problem keeping my mouth shut.

When I did open my mouth, I was slapped. I concluded that I got what I deserved, because I had disobeyed what I thought were God's instructions for battered wives. It was years before I realized that while it would have been wise at times for me to hold my tongue, Sonny had no right to hit me when I failed to stifle my words. Abuse of any kind is never justified, but it took a long time for me to see that.

By 1984 I was attending church every time the doors were open. In addition to regular church services I attended Bible conferences, Bible studies—you name it, I was there. I was a changed woman. I followed the teachings of such men as James Robison and Milton Green. I was so hungry for the things of God!

There was one Bible verse that kept coming to my mind night and day: "Do the work of an evangelist..." I wanted to do the work of an evangelist; I just didn't know how. I wanted to tell others about Jesus and how much God loved them. I wanted to let everyone know that their sins could be washed clean, because Jesus died on the cross for them.

Exposed Heart

In the midst of my frustration, an idea came to me. Sonny had bought motorcycles for everyone in the family. Ann and Howard were too young to ride their own, so Sonny put Howard on the back of his, and Ann rode with Charlsey.

I stuffed the side pouch of my motorcycle with pamphlets that told how to have a personal relationship with Jesus. I placed them in telephone booths, on park benches, in gas station rest rooms. Moments when I felt especially bold, I'd place them directly into people's hands.

Handing out tracts was like sowing seeds of hope and love in people's hearts. As St. Francis of Assisi said, "Preach the gospel all the time; if necessary use words." That's how I wanted to live. I decided to practice my faith in spite of Sonny's disapproval. Demonstrating God's love toward others became a lifestyle for me as my faith and boldness grew stronger.

No matter how hard I tried, I could not close up the chasm between Sonny and me. The sense of urgency I felt to share the truth of Jesus with others further crippled our marriage. Going to Christian meetings through the week and then sleeping with a man who was not willing to change his lifestyle created a void in my soul. I prayed, "God, I'd give up everything if You would change Sonny's heart."

Riding motorcycles, visiting amusement parks, and eating out at our favorite restaurants gave people the impression that we were a model family. We may have been able to fool the world into thinking that everything was fine. But my heart now belonged totally to Jesus, and there was no turning back.

Chapter Thirteen

Second Chances

It was a dream come true. My husband wanted to serve the Lord as much as I did. We began to read the Bible together in the evenings. The children were able to share their faith without fear of ridicule. We were a team. But my security blanket unraveled overnight when Sonny told me that he was giving up his newfound faith. I braced myself for the inevitable.

In the spring of 1984 Sonny began a new business venture. He bought a plant nursery in Tyler, Texas, a two-and-a-half hour drive east from Dallas. This required him to be gone days at a time. He would bring home these gorgeous plants, as plush and green as our flourishing marriage. However, I pitied all those plants. God knows I wasn't born with a green thumb, and as much as I hate to admit it, most of them wilted and died. Plastic plants were the only things I couldn't kill. Sometimes I wondered if even they were safe.

I kept a watchful eye on the kitchen clock waiting for Sonny to walk in the front door. I had plans. Big plans.

Exposed Heart

The shrill sound of the phone caught me off guard, and I jumped to my feet. It was Sonny. "Honey, something has come up, and I won't be able to come home until morning. You know how crazy this job can be."

I let out a disappointed sigh, as my plans deflated like a balloon. I stared at the clock on the kitchen wall. Something wasn't right in the tone of his voice, and I had a funny feeling about our brief conversation.

I made arrangements for the kids to be cared for and drove to Tyler, pulling into the hotel parking lot at eleven o'clock that night. I went to the hotel manager and asked for the key to my husband's room. Well, a manager is *never, ever* supposed to hand out a key to anyone the way he did, and why he did it I'll never know. I thanked him and went to Sonny's room. The lights were off, and the room was empty.

Knowing my husband as I did, I figured he was sitting at a bar laughing and talking with the locals. The town isn't very big, so I drove up and down the main street looking for his car until about midnight. My back ached, and I felt a headache coming on as I grudgingly pulled my car back into the hotel parking lot. I dug the key from my purse and made my way to his room. I turned the knob and opened the door. The lights were off. An ominous silence blanketed the room.

I stepped in and blinked hard to adjust to the darkness. I saw two shadowy figures snuggling on the couch. They each held a drink in their hands. When they noticed my presence, their bodies stirred and changed positions quickly. My eyes made out the two figures. One was a young college girl who worked at the nursery, and the other was Sonny. She was the very girl who had laughed with me and befriended me when we did a commercial together for the company.

I was livid!

Guilt painted their faces when they realized it was me. "It's...it's not what you think. Really," Sonny stuttered. I gritted my teeth and made a beeline to my parked car.

Sonny chased me.

I remembered the gun sitting under the front seat of the car. I thought to myself, *I'm going to kill him...I'm going to kill both of them!*

I was inches away from grabbing the gun when I heard what was unmistakably the voice of God, *Vengeance is Mine. I will repay!*

I froze.

I couldn't move a muscle. I couldn't reach for the gun. Fear, rage, and disappointment paralyzed me.

Sonny reached the car—and me. But he was caught off guard when a man came running toward us. This stranger hurled himself at Sonny and knocked him to the ground. As they scuffled, I ran back to the hotel room.

I believe God sent this stranger to protect me from Sonny. I knew beyond a shadow of a doubt that a beating was coming my way; I just wasn't sure when. The stranger's intervention spared me from an enraged husband.

I ran back into the hotel room and locked the door. The girl was on the phone. "Please, please come pick me up," she cried into the receiver.

All sanity left me at that moment. Rage and jealousy raced through my body. I pulled off my shoe and unmercifully beat her over the head and in the face with the spike of the heel. She dropped the phone and screamed, "He's not my old man. I've got my own old man!"

I yelled back, "This is what you get for being in the room with my husband! You knew he was married to me! You know me!"

Her blood-soaked hair stuck to her forehead and cheeks as she kept pleading for me to stop. She covered her face with her hands.

It must have been the hand of the Lord that kept me from killing her, because I stopped just short of knocking her unconscious. I walked out of the room and drove home. I was glad I had caught him. As far as I was concerned our marriage was over.

I thanked God for intervening. I was relieved that I hadn't killed them both. They weren't worth losing my children over. If God had not stopped me, I would have blown them away. I later heard that she had to have more than a hundred stitches in her head and face. I was sorry for what I had done. I prayed that night for God to forgive me.

It's ironic that I could do such a terrible thing to this girl at a time in my life when I was trying to serve God. I did this horrible thing after totally surrendering my life to Jesus. It frustrated me that I couldn't trust myself or my emotions.

One Sunday afternoon Sonny called to tell me the good news: He had been watching a television preacher and had asked Jesus into his heart!

I hung up on him.

Sonny called back, "I mean it, Jackie! I *really* did. I asked Jesus into my heart."

"That's the lowest, dirtiest thing you could have ever done to me. All these years I've wanted this more than anything in the world. And for you to use that now is the sorriest thing I've ever heard!"

I hung up the phone a second time.

And then God spoke, *"I've forgiven you for so much, and he's saying that he's repented. You're not even going to give him a second chance and forgive him, when I've been so merciful to you?"*

The words stung. All those prayers I had prayed asking God to change my husband now mocked me. Demons taunted me. *You can't forgive him. You have to keep your dignity. You've done nothing wrong; now is your chance to leave.*

The soothing voice of the enemy sounded right to me. Sonny didn't deserve one ounce of forgiveness from me; yet, the Holy Spirit continued to convict my heart. I searched deep in the crevices of my soul and admitted I wanted to obey the Lord, but I didn't believe I could forget the memory of that girl in the hotel room.

The truth is I was jealous of her. She was this young girl with breasts the size of Dolly Parton's, and I'm sure they were real. Her face wasn't all that pretty, but with a body like hers it didn't matter! One look in the mirror told me that youth was passing me by quickly. After three babies my body was not the same, and the years of abuse and stress had left me with a crooked nose and small but visible creases around my eyes. Makeup could give the illusion of youth, but I knew my best years were behind me.

The phone rang a third time.

"I swear it, Jackie. I'm going to live for God," he promised.

I took a deep breath. "OK, you can come home. We'll get through this somehow," I answered.

Over the next year Sonny's life turned around. Our whole family went to church each Sunday. Sonny almost wore out his Bible from reading it so much. He even gave scripture memory assignments to each member of the family. It seemed as if we always had an assignment. I believe Charlsey memorized hundreds of scriptures over that year. Mike couldn't memorize, so he listened to Bible tapes. Everyone who set foot into the Holland house got a sermon from Sonny. He preached to everyone, even the mailman! Sonny broke off all ties with his old buddies and quit his job.

It was a dream come true.

The dream was short-lived when Sonny unexpectedly walked away from his commitment to serve the Lord. He had a sharp business mind and was a born salesman. Unfortunately, he didn't know how to integrate his Christianity with his business skills.

After paying the bills one afternoon he said, "Jackie, I can't make any money and be a Christian at the same time. I've decided that I'm going to make money."

Sonny stopped going to church and reading his Bible. A week later he left Texas to work for an oil company in another state. Within a year Sonny founded his own oil company and made a small fortune. He eventually bought his own plane and rental property. He bought about thirty thoroughbred horses and stabled them in fancy horse hotels.

Once a month Sonny came to town and stayed for the weekend. It was nothing for him to dole out hundred-dollar bills to each of the kids and then leave as quickly as he had arrived.

I filled the emptiness by staying busy. Charlsey had been away attending Bible college in Springfield, Missouri, where she met her future husband. The first time I met him I wanted to shout for joy. He was everything I wanted for my daughter. It blessed me to plan her wedding, maybe because my experiences with marriage had been so unpleasant. Pouring my soul into Charlsey's wedding, I believe, brought a measure of healing to my past wounds. Between planning my daughter's wedding and pursuing my passion for God, I managed to fill the empty spaces in my life.

I hungered for a more intimate relationship with my heavenly Father. I watched Christian television around the clock, I was in church every time the doors were open, and I owned every Bible teaching syllabus that I could get my hands on. I can't count the number of tapes I received each month from various ministries. I was reading my Bible and praying. I had a prayer list a mile long.

As much as I enjoyed learning about God, it was putting my beliefs into practice that gave me the most fulfillment. I took seriously the biblical definition of "pure" religion: feeding the hungry, clothing the naked, and caring for orphans and widows. I was driven to fulfill this call.

I started out by accepting responsibility for the food closet at Evangel Temple. I was in charge of stocking the closet with non-perishable food items and organizing them. It was not a hard job by any means. The closet was exactly that, a closet. It was no bigger than the small walk-in closet in my bedroom. But it held food and met a need. I was honored to be in charge of something that I knew pleased God, even if it was small.

I must have looked silly praying over every can, every bag of beans. I prayed for God to bless and nourish the people that received the food. I asked God to reveal His love to them. I prayed for their salvation.

Around the holidays I volunteered to distribute food and clothing to the poor at a local shelter. This experience tugged at my heartstrings. It stirred something deep inside me, something that I had no idea was there.

At night I couldn't get the faces of the people out of my mind. A crying baby riding his mother's hip, a little boy in a tattered shirt, a little girl in a too-big dress, stained and wrinkled. Faces weathered by years of pain and poverty. I wanted to wrap my arms around the people and tell them the story of God's love for them, the greatest story of all. In meeting the needs of hurting people, I began to find fulfillment and meaning for my life.

Working as a volunteer, doing something I enjoyed, filled my days. I experienced sadness and joy at the same time as I handed out food. Some moments brought laughter, as was the case one time when I took off my shoes because my feet were aching.

When it was time to go home, I discovered my shoes were missing! I looked everywhere, but they were nowhere in sight. I laughed as I drove home barefoot, imagining my beautiful shoes being worn by someone who got more than food that day.

Charlsey's wedding day arrived. I was both ecstatic and relieved to see my daughter growing up to be a woman after God's own heart. I cried buckets of tears as I watched my daughter, this beautiful bride, walk down the aisle and exchange vows with a godly man.

These were growing times for me. For years I'd begged God to change Sonny, because I believed that my happiness and my self-worth depended on what men thought of me. But God did something better. He drew me into His loving arms and began to show me that Jesus could meet all of my needs. God loved me enough to rescue me from the lie that said my value came from man. In His kindness, He didn't change the people and circumstances around me.

He changed me.

Chapter Fourteen

Hidden Treasures

The room began to spin as I leaned against the bathroom wall using my arms and hands to avoid the kicks and punches. It was no use. I slumped to the tiled floor and curled into a fetal position as the blows came down harder and harder. Blood ran from my nose onto my sequined evening dress, the one that had promised to make me look slender and glamorous. The loud curses drowned out my cry for help. I couldn't believe this was happening again.

I was now thirty-nine, and my marriage to Sonny was stagnant. Except for an occasional slap across my cheek, he had stopped beating me, although he continued his verbal abuse. He regularly threatened to leave, but he never did.

Until the day of a relative's wedding, I had no reason to fear Sonny anymore. I knew the routine well. Act happy. Make it look as if Sonny and I had a picture-perfect marriage. He made me promise to not act religious and embarrass him. I kept my promise. In fact, I danced the night away at the reception and even celebrated with a couple of glasses of wine.

The crowd had thinned, so we decided to head up to our room. I was relaxed and happy, and I wasn't pretending. Sonny closed the door and bolted it; I slumped flirtatiously against the breakfast counter. Sonny's face turned hard, and he glared across the room at me. A twinge of fear crawled up my spine.

The beast was back with a vengeance. To this day I do not know why he chose to beat me with such brutality. Time stood still as he kicked me with the pointed toe of a cowboy boot, leaving black and blue bruises up and down my side and on my arms and legs. He pummeled my face with his fists. He threw me against the bathroom wall; I crouched down on the floor and curled my arms and legs into a fetal position until his rage subsided.

I whimpered and groaned like a wounded, bleeding animal until the cursing and hammering fists stopped. I prayed for God to let me live. It was the worst beating Sonny had ever inflicted on me. I kept asking myself, *What did I do wrong? Why is he doing this to me?*

That was the last time Sonny beat me. Like a horrible nightmare, the beating became a surreal memory I kept to myself and never spoke about. I buried the beating in my mind and vowed it would never happen again. I sometimes wondered if the explosion of rage he exhibited in the hotel room satisfied a subconscious urge for revenge. Maybe it was his way of getting back at me for shooting him or for interrupting his rendezvous with the sexy employee from the nursery. Maybe it was prompted by the guilt he was carrying for having an affair with the young woman he was seeing. I must have done something to incite his pent-up fury. Somehow, it had to be my fault.

Life changed for me after that night. I continued to play the part of the committed wife, but my heart was closed to him. And I continued to live with his taunting but hollow threats to leave.

Our marriage survived for the most part because Sonny began several new business ventures around the country that kept him away for weeks at a time. He was up to his elbows in business deals and doing well. Money was no concern, and for a season it brought comfort and pleasure, in spite of our lousy marriage.

The weekends Sonny spent at home were surprisingly enjoyable. He became Prince Charming as he pampered us with gifts and entertained us with stories from his latest travels around Texas and other parts of the country. He was usually in a good mood, and we got along. We laughed and enjoyed one another's company. In a way it was like playing house, because we didn't have to deal with the day-to-day irritants in each other's personalities. There were no arguments to work out, no financial stresses. If there was a disagreement, Sonny was back on the road before the tension could take its toll.

It's not hard to be on your best behavior when you see someone only once a month. The weekends were always a whirlwind of entertainment and so-called family time. I'm sure that it meant something to the children to have their father around. They adored him. But as for me, I was living a lie.

I knew it. Sonny knew it.

But there was no reason for either of us to abandon the marriage. As long as my husband was on the road more than he was at home, I felt comfortable with the arrangement. I prayed all the time that God would change his heart and make him the godly husband I dreamed of having.

In the fall of 1985 I left Evangel Temple after a church split that left many people hurt and disillusioned, including me. My very existence depended on being with other believers. My life revolved around Jesus Christ and the fellowship of others who also followed Him.

For me, Christianity wasn't about a set of rules. It had everything to do with a relationship with God—a relationship that Sonny resented. I was tired of living a double life, and I promised myself to never again hide my relationship with Jesus.

Desperate for a church family, I learned about a group of people who met regularly on Sunday at a school gymnasium near my home. I decided to visit. The minute I stepped through the doors, I knew I had found my spiritual family.

When the pastor, Doug White, asked if any one had a need, one man stood up and said, "My wife needs a washing machine. Ours broke down and I'm unable to fix it, and we don't have the money for even a used one. We've been trusting God."

Across the aisle a woman stood and waved her hand in the air. "I have a washing machine I can give you."

As the meeting wore on, more and more needs were met as people asked and other people gave. I thought, *Now this is real Christianity!*

The church was named Lake Country-Midcities, which later changed to Restoration. The growing congregation eventually moved from the gymnasium to a vacant shopping center just a few miles from my home.

While we were still meeting at the high school I scheduled an appointment with the pastor. I was nervous as I sat in his office, hoping that I'd find the words to express what was going on inside my heart. "I just want to do God's work. I want to clothe the naked, feed the hungry, help hurting women..." I tried to explain.

Brother Doug looked at me with concerned, loving eyes and began to pray in a gentle voice, "God, it's apparent that You're doing a work in Jackie's life, so I just ask You to bring the resources and the people together to help her do the job that You've called her to do. She cares about hurting and broken people. I know You're doing this in her, and so I ask You to bring her the help that she needs to be able to get this done. Amen."

There was nothing earth-shattering about his prayer, but I felt as if a fountain of faith and hope had erupted in my heart. Tears spilled from my eyes. I knew the pastor's words had touched God's heart.

Around this time the economy had become unsteady. The oil industry suffered a major blow, and gas prices skyrocketed. Many of our friends in the real estate business went bankrupt. It was a time of economic disaster for us and others who had their wealth stored up in land and oil deals.

I began supplementing our meager income by buying and reselling valuables that I collected on my daily scavenger hunts at estate and garage sales. It became my morning ritual to spread the classified section of the newspaper across the kitchen table beside my steaming cup of coffee while I scanned the columns for a good deal. I circled phone numbers and spent the next several hours with my ear to the phone.

Each morning I viewed the classified ads as more or less a grown-up version of my childhood treasure hunts. I'd find all kinds of great deals on jewelry, antiques, and furs. I was like a little mouse scurrying around town in my gold Mercedes station wagon, packing it full of stuff.

It gave me an adrenaline rush to wheel and deal. Bargaining was in my blood. I knew how to spot a good deal. I could see the hidden value in an item. What one person saw as a piece of junk I could sometimes turn around and sell for twice what I paid for it. I especially enjoyed dealing in antiques and jewelry.

One time God used a particularly funny phone call to teach me a lesson on riches. I dialed the phone number listed in an intriguing ad.

"I'm calling about your diamond ring listed in today's newspaper," I said after a woman answered.

The owner described the diamond in such detail that by the time she had finished, I was licking my chops! I couldn't wait to get my hands on her gem.

"Why on earth are you selling such a valuable ring?" I asked her.

She answered, "Honey, I'm fifty-eight years old. When I was your age I used to love to get all dressed up in my party clothes and jewelry and go dancing. It was fun."

I smiled. This was my kind of woman!

Then came the baited hook. "Listen, honey. At my age there is only one thing that is important."

"What's that?" I asked, bewildered.

She chuckled. "Having a good b.m. [bowel movement] every day!"

I gave a polite laugh, but truthfully I failed to see the humor in her punch line. Appearances and expensive things were still important to me. I was conditioned to believe that things meant love, which of course is a lie. I believed if I could fill my life with things, then I would feel loved—that is, until it broke or the newness wore off. Then I had to replace my "thing" with something newer and more expensive. Now that I am over fifty years old the significance of her poignant response has become clearer to me.

As the weeks and months crept by with no hope in sight that the economy would shift gears, Sonny became more and more determined to beat the odds. He ventured out in other areas of business while the rest of us did what we could to chip in. The financial crunch took its toll on all of us as we fought to keep our heads above water.

One thing was certain—Sonny was no quitter! He kept his chin up during those rough months, and I never doubted for a moment that he would pull us out of this financial rut. My happiness depended on it.

During this hard time God began teaching me a series of life lessons. I learned that my security couldn't be bound up in riches. Money was like a god to me. It was my source of security. For the first time in my life I was learning to depend on God for my daily bread.

I began to see the greater treasure that God had promised me. As I pondered my pastor's prayer I remembered the faces of some of the people I had encountered since surrendering my life to serve the Lord.

A woman in my weekly Bible study asked me to visit the jail with her. I kept putting her off with trivial excuses. I'm not sure why; maybe I could identify too closely with the women behind bars.

My excuses didn't deter this woman one bit. Week after week she invited me to go with her to the jail. Finally, I consented. It was the only way I knew to shut her up! However, the joke was on me.

Exposed Heart

The moment I saw the women in the jail I knew that I was going to be a part of the jail ministry. One evening after ministering to the inmates I shared with them just how much they meant to me. As they began to understand how much God loved them and how special our times together were to me, some began to cry. It blessed me to know that God could use someone like me, despite all my failures.

Chapter Fifteen

First Fruits

A cluster of grapes in the hands of my youngest son changed the course of my life. I still get misty-eyed when I remember Father's Day in 1987 when my heavenly Father revealed a piece of my destiny in the most unlikely way.

Sonny was in town for Father's Day, and we planned to take my father on an afternoon fishing trip. He loved fishing. While the men sorted rods and reels and went to get bait, my mother and I scrambled around grabbing sunscreen, hats, and all the stuff that men don't usually think about.

It was a beautiful, sunny day. I had just stepped onto the front porch when my youngest son, Howard, and his friend walked up. They looked like a couple of fat-cheeked chipmunks suspiciously stuffing the largest grapes I'd ever seen into their already full mouths. Pleasure painted their faces as the plump grapes exploded inside their overstuffed mouths.

I propped my hands on my hips and gave them my stern-mother face. "Where on earth did you get those grapes?" I asked.

Howard dangled them by the stem. Still chomping, he answered, "You'll never believe it, Mom. They're in the dumpster behind the grocery store."

"Oh, really?" I asked, still a little suspicious of these two twelve-year-olds.

These were no ordinary grapes by any means. They were plump, luscious, and purple—not the kind you'd find at your run-of-the-mill neighborhood fruit stand. These were the kind served on a sterling-silver tray at a four-star restaurant.

Howard flashed his charming smile and waved his arm for me to follow. "Come on, I'll show you," he said.

Overcome with curiosity, I followed the boys to the dumpster behind a specialty store near my parents' house. I peered inside the giant bin, and sure enough there were all kinds of fruits and vegetables, some still in the boxes crammed in the giant trash bin. I couldn't believe that someone could throw away anything so perfect!

I instructed the boys to stay there while I went back to the house for my car. I returned a few moments later. If any of the neighbors were watching, my mother would have been so embarrassed trying to explain what her daughter was doing pulling food from the trash!

The boys and I hoisted box after box out of the dumpster and loaded them into the back of my car. Rescuing the beautiful food took precedence over the fishing trip. My heart pounded wildly as I pictured myself distributing the food to people who lived in the run-down apartment complex behind our church's meeting place. I'd found treasure in the trash, and I knew just what to do with it!

Life is so full of contrasts. I'll never understand how life can deal us victories and defeats sometimes in the same day. "It was the best of times, it was the worst of times," Dickens wrote in his classic novel *A Tale of Two Cities*. His words certainly applied to my life.

I don't remember much about the fishing trip that day. My heart was still racing when I climbed into the passenger seat of my car to head home. Sonny was at the wheel when I put my hand inside a pocket on the passenger door and pulled out a crinkled bingo card. I turned it over and noticed Sonny's name written next to a woman's name, with the same address and telephone number written below. Disappointment and anger swept over me.

"Who is this woman?" I demanded.

Sonny brushed it off. "Oh, that's the name of this man's daughter I've been working on a business deal with down in Houston. It's nothing," he answered casually.

I stiffened. "I don't believe you," I said.

Sonny pointed a finger at me and warned, "Don't you dare go and embarrass me. This is an important deal that will mean a lot to our family. It's nothing more than that."

I clutched the card tighter. "I'm going to call," I insisted.

"Don't you dare," he warned.

I'm not sure why I waited a full day to make the call. Maybe I wanted the whole thing to magically go away. I'd had suspicions that there had been other women since the incident with the buxom blond I almost clobbered to death with my shoe, but they were just that—suspicions.

Now the evidence stared back at me and dared me to ignore it. A part of me wanted to sweep this under the carpet, as I had done so many other times. However, this was more than a gut feeling. I knew this one couldn't be ignored.

I was in the shower when it dawned on me that Sonny would try to call the girl to corroborate their stories. I kept the water running as I carefully picked up the phone to eavesdrop. Just as I suspected they were talking in hushed tones discussing a way to wriggle out of their predicament.

Suddenly, I felt like the guilty party intruding on a private conversation. I had to quickly remind myself that I wasn't guilty of anything. I hated the fact that my mind played those games on me, always convincing me that I was the problem. It was always my fault, not his.

I carefully lowered the receiver and went to find the bingo card. Of course, it was gone. Sonny was always good at destroying the evidence, but I'd been down this road too many times, and I knew to write the number down where he wouldn't find it. I called the girl's number when Sonny was out of the house. It was no surprise to me that her story matched Sonny's.

"Mr. Holland was in town..." she began.

It sickened me to hear her refer to Sonny as Mr. Holland, if indeed she was sleeping with him. I kept listening.

"I'm in college, and I was just visiting my dad over the weekend. I ended up playing bingo with my dad's friends. I don't know why you're worried," she said.

Though she could never fully explain why her name was on the bingo card, I hung up the phone, wanting to believe the lie.

When Sonny was away from the house I did some more detective work and found a printout from a multi-level marketing company Sonny worked for on the side. Her name and his were listed side by side on a giant printout, followed by the same address and phone number. The proof that they lived together in Houston was there in black and white. The truth stabbed my heart like a knife.

When Sonny returned home I waved the printout in front of his face. "I know you're lying!" I cried.

Sonny rolled his eyes. "You're crazy!" he fumed.

"I'm sick of all your lies! I'm going to talk to everyone I can until I find the whole truth!" I threatened.

"Don't you dare!"

I looked him square in the eyes and said, "If you'll pray with me right now and tell me in the presence of God that you want this marriage, I'll let this whole thing go and never mention it again. All you have to do is pray here and now."

I would have given anything for him to do just that. Sonny may have been many things, but he wasn't a hypocrite. He lowered his head. "I can't do that," he answered.

"Then it's over," I said firmly.

Cold silence blanketed the room. There was nothing left to say.

Sonny left the room and packed his bags. I had no fight left in me. Hot tears spilled from my eyes as I buried my face in a pillow to muffle the sobs.

Once the truth brought the lies to light, I could no longer live with my husband's infidelity. Sonny moved in with his out-of-town girlfriend, and that was the end of our marriage. I later found out that she was pregnant.

It broke my heart because I loved him and I wanted our marriage to work. I'd invested fifteen years of my life into the marriage, and now it was over.

Sonny was saddened, too. As much as he despised me, at times I know he found security in the idea of having a wife and family, but his need to be with this woman was the driving wedge that tore us apart. He could no longer have the best of both worlds.

We officially divorced a year later. This time, I faced an awkward transition from married to single. Unlike the other times I was divorced, this time my children were older, with my role as their guardian and sole nurturer diminished. Charlsey was married and living in another city. Little Sonny went to live with his dad. Ann went to her mother. Mike graduated from high school and held down a job as a groundskeeper. He and Howard decided to live with me.

While I was thankful for my sons' companionship, as hard as I tried I couldn't shake the feelings of depression. Daily I battled the invisible giant that threatened to suck the life from me and then swallow me whole. Loneliness, I discovered, is a silent demon that gnaws at a person's soul.

God saw my need, and He brought a godly woman into my life to begin healing my heart. Larie White, Pastor Doug's wife, asked me to spend one day a week with her as she ran errands and shopped. The other six days Larie spent caring for her ninety-two-year-old mother, who was confined to a wheelchair and needed daily supervision.

Here was a woman who could be doing her own thing but unselfishly chose to give of herself to care for her mother. And she wanted to spend her one day off with me! I was both honored and a little confused about why she would want me to tag along, since she was happily married and I was miserably single.

They say laughter is medicine for the soul. If that is the case, then I got dose after dose on our weekly outings. We would laugh at the silliest things! Larie could find humor in anything, and I laughed right along. She'd have me doubled over laughing at a funny face she made while trying on a ridiculous hat, and then she would regain her composure and share a life-changing word with me or begin praying for whatever was on her heart...right in the store!

I learned so much in the year we spent together. I found that I could have fun, look beautiful, and be a Christian at the same time. There was freedom in Larie's Christian walk. Freedom from religious rules. Freedom from the expectations of others. Larie simply lived out her faith wherever she was—at church, in the grocery store, at the mall, or at home. I saw in her a woman of integrity. I found in her a mentor and a friend.

Although much healing came during my times with Larie, she couldn't totally fill the void that was left in my heart after the divorce. Like the boxes of fruit and vegetables in the trash bin, I too felt like a discarded commodity, replaced by youth and beauty. I wanted my heavenly Father to look into the trash bin of my life with all of its mistakes and failures and find something of value.

I needed God to rescue me.

Chapter Sixteen

Small Beginnings

A trash bin seemed an unlikely place to begin a food ministry, but then a stable seemed an unlikely place to birth a king. As gnats buzzed around my head and the stench turned my stomach, I clung to the words from the Bible as my hope for greater things to come: "Despise not small beginnings." I held these words in my heart as I began my daily mission of delivering food to the hungry.

I put on a fresh pot of coffee; the aroma alone helped clear the grogginess from my head. After my divorce, the loneliness and heartache I felt left a void in my heart and a longing for companionship and love. The trash bin of food, on the other hand, offered a reason much bigger than myself to crawl out of bed and resist the temptation to cover my problems with a blanket over my head. A deep call to feed the hungry had settled in my soul, and I had no choice but to fulfill it.

My car was loaded down with fruit as I steered into the parking lot of Pine Hollow, an apartment building behind my church. Sunday after Sunday in my rush to get to church on time, I couldn't help but notice the children who spent their Sunday mornings playing in the concrete parking lot. A tin can scored points instead of a ball. Men sat outside their apartments trying to escape the stifling summer heat. Mothers with flushed faces fanned crying babies.

A chain-link fence separated the apartments from the church property, making it appear as if someone was trying to keep others out, or worse, to fence us in. The irony seared my conscience like a branding iron. How could I praise God while people only a few yards away not know the great love that God has for each of us? Didn't the Bible affirm that true religion was to feed the hungry and clothe the naked and to take care of the widows and orphans?

I turned off the ignition. And I prayed.

It was an ordinary summer day when I first ventured to Pine Hollow Apartments. As I drove up, a lady was standing in her doorway. She looked back at me with listless eyes. Her brown hair tumbled in uncombed strands over her thin shoulders. Tiny children were wrapped around her legs and dangled from her arms. I held up a bunch of bananas. "Would you like some fruit and vegetables?" I asked.

"Oh, I don't have any money," she answered.

"You don't need money," I explained, excitedly. "It's free. It's from the Lord. He wants you to have them!"

Her lips quivered. "I just fed my children the last of our food this morning. I told them there was nothing left to eat."

Her eyes brimmed with tears as she allowed me to haul box after box of food into her cramped kitchen. There was barely enough room in her small refrigerator to store the food. A wave of sheer exhilaration penetrated every bone in my body. I was experiencing firsthand what Jesus meant when He told His disciples, "It is more joyful to give than to receive."

Leaving the parking lot, I watched in my rearview mirror as children danced and laughed while shoving bananas into their already full mouths. Banana peels littered the sky as the children pitched them into the air with squeals of delight. It is a picture permanently etched in my mind.

On my second trip to the garbage bin I insisted that Mike and Howard go with me. I assured myself that climbing into a garbage bin wasn't a felony, but I felt safer with my sons standing guard as I rescued more fruit. I tried not to think about what I would do if one of my parents' many neighbors spotted me climbing in and out of the garbage. I could only imagine the rumors it would start!

My car was packed, and I barely had enough room for myself, much less for my two sons. While Mike and Howard walked back to my parents' house, I drove to the same apartments I had visited the day before. It only made sense to knock on the same door where I had planted the boxes full of fruit on the first day of my mission.

This time the doe-eyed young woman didn't answer. I found myself standing face-to-face with one of the harshest looking men I've ever encountered. His hair was matted, and he was so thin that I could see his ribs. He stood guard at the door as I tried to peek around and spy on the children I had seen the day before.

"I've brought you more fruit and vegetables," I said, trying my best to stay calm in spite of the millions of butterflies in my stomach.

An awkward silence set in like a heavy fog. I glanced at the apartment number mounted on the door. I was in the right place. With fire in his eyes he asked, "Why are you doing this?"

I cleared my throat. "I'm bringing you food because God told me to do this. He loves you." I answered.

Our eyes locked. For a split second I felt like running for my life. *Oh, God, please protect me. Give me favor with this man,* I prayed silently.

Almost immediately the glare from his eyes softened, and his scowl disappeared. Without warning, tears threatened to spill from his eyes. At that instant God gave me a glimpse in to this stranger's heart. He was a wounded child inside a grown man's body, in need of love and affirmation. His needs were no different from mine.

Tears began to fall as he gazed at his unlikely visitor. I cried too. God had broken through this man's rough exterior in the simplest of ways. An act of kindness and a loving word had touched his heart.

The young woman joined him in the doorway. She nudged his arm. "I told you that God speaks to some people," she said.

The food delivery became an everyday occurrence. I was able to take food to others in the apartment building, as well as to laundromats. Sometimes the food I was delivering went straight from the trunk of my car into a bystander's hands. Those days brought such joy and satisfaction to my soul that the emptiness inside me was filled as I shared the goodness of God's provision with hungry people.

Mike gave me his old red '76 Pontiac after he bought himself a pickup. Unfortunately, when Sonny left town, he borrowed my car—permanently. I fussed and fumed for weeks after he left with my gold Mercedes. How I hated myself for letting Sonny have my only reliable piece of transportation!

One day I heard the Lord ask, *"Jackie, are you willing to sell everything you have and give it to the poor?"*

"Yes, Lord," I replied.

Suddenly, I realized the significance of God's question. This wasn't about losing my car. It was a lesson on being willing to let everything go—not only my physical possessions but my emotional ties as well. In order to serve God fully, I had to be willing to give away or sell everything I had.

My visits to the dumpster became routine. As summer approached, the ordeal of climbing in and out of the trash bin in the Texas heat made my skin clammy with perspiration. My clothes clung to my body like wet rags. Sweat dripped from my forehead. I am sure I was a sight! Sylvia, then a volunteer and now my secretary, held my legs and feet as I bent inside the dumpster to retrieve the produce. It never occurred to me that I might encounter rats, which I have always viewed with horror. I did, however, pray that the Lord would not allow me to find a baby that had been abandoned and left to die.

After each visit to the dumpster I'd go home and bathe and put on a fresh set of clothes. God never required this of me; it simply was something I wanted to do. I was God's representative to people who may never have heard the good news that God loved them, so I wanted to look and smell my best.

Trusting God became my lifestyle. I never got a penny for child support, and I had no savings to fall back on. I had little time for chasing down deals in the classified ads while I was pouring myself into feeding the hungry. I sold my furs, jewelry, and furniture to help make ends meet. I ate the same food from the garbage bin that I was sharing with others. I was on a quest of faith as I learned to follow God's leading.

There were days when I had enough food to feed an army. And I would ask God, "Where do I go today? Do I turn left or right?"

As I learned to hear God's voice, a pattern emerged. One day of the week I delivered food to the apartments. Other days God would direct me to a laundromat. It seemed to work out that I would deliver around the same time, at the same place, week after week. People would be waiting with empty boxes and grocery bags, their hearts full of anticipation.

Within minutes the food would be gone. I didn't need to preach or to pass out Christian literature. I shared the love of God simply by bringing food to these hungry, hurting people.

One day, as I was preparing to dig through the dumpster, I heard the Lord speak to me. He told me to wear my best clothes and approach the manager of the store about picking up the food before he threw it away. It sounded like a good idea to me! I had grown weary of climbing into the trash day after day. The very thought of getting the food before it was discarded gave me a much-needed burst of energy.

I put on my finest clothes and my best jewelry, and approached the store manager. He greeted me with a firm handshake. I tried my best to hide my nervousness, although a hundred butterflies fluttered inside me. "Every day I come to your store and pull out food from the garbage bin to feed hungry people," I explained.

His expression betrayed a mixture of sheer confusion and shock as if it had never occurred to him that anyone would want to eat food from a trash bin. I understood his confusion. He most likely lived in an affluent neighborhood, without a clue that a few miles from his home people were poor and hungry.

I took a deep breath and asked point-blank, "May I pick up your discarded food before you throw it away?" I asked.

The storeowner stared at me with puzzled eyes. He paused and rubbed his chin. "I guess it'll be all right. I'll just set the food aside. As long as you come and get it, it's all yours," he declared.

I bit my tongue as a cheer of joy erupted in my spirit. We shook hands, and it was a done deal. My heart pounded with enthusiasm as I returned to my car. Once inside I could no longer contain my emotions. I shouted praises to God all the way home.

It wasn't long before God told me to approach other store managers with the same confidence. To my amazement, they responded as the first one had. No one had ever approached them with this kind of request before, but now that I had, they were more than willing to help out.

We received food from several specialty stores similar to the one near my parents' home. It was nothing to walk away with fancy cheesecakes, gourmet coffee, and all the cakes and pies one could imagine. Sometimes I was given choice cuts of meat like sirloins and T-bone steaks ready for the grill. The only problem was that I had no cooling system to keep the meat fresh. It was all I could do to give away cuts of sirloins and T-bones fast enough!

I was slowly building a roster of stores. As the list grew, so did my need for more workers and a bigger vehicle. My little car could no longer hold all the food given to me by local grocery stores. My prayer for a vehicle was answered when a man named Jerry Edmondson donated his van to the food ministry. It was an older van that had no heat or air-conditioning. But it was still God's provision, and I received it as gratefully as if I'd just been given a BMW. In fact, my friend Sylvia called it God's Chariot.

In the winter months I dressed in sweaters and piled blankets over my legs as I shivered on my various food-delivery routes. In the summer I would dress as modestly as I could, roll the windows down, and drive a little faster. As hard as I tried not to let the heat get to me, it always did.

When I complained, God reminded me of the winter our family lived on greasy sausages when I was a child and the lesson I learned about being thankful in all situations. "Give thanks for what you do have, and pray about what you need," my father always told me. Measuring God's provision not by human standards but by spiritual supply allowed me to see things in a brand-new light.

During one of my trips to the laundromat, I was taken aback by the voice of a small girl who looked up at me with wistful eyes. "Are you an angel?" she asked.

Her face radiated with innocence and hope. I hated to disappoint her, but I had to be truthful. "No, I'm not an angel. But I am God's child, and I'm here to tell you that God loves you."

I don't think I ever convinced this child that I was anything less than a celestial creation sent to feed her family at the local laundromat. Her bright, innocent eyes captured the message of God's love in spite of who I was or wasn't.

The fruit and vegetables were merely the means through which an invisible, omnipotent God could touch ordinary people; the awesome essence of Almighty God could be transferred to a small child through a yielded human vessel like me. Looking into the eyes of that child and realizing I was God's messenger of hope was one of the most fulfilling events of my life.

Chapter Seventeen

The Dream

It started out as a night like any other. I had fallen asleep after an exhausting workday and tossed and turned as a dream unfolded. Images of a disfigured baby and the disheartening sighs of the crowd caused me to toss and turn on my bed. It was a dream unlike any I had dreamed before. I anxiously waited to hear what God was saying to me.

In its early stages, the food ministry must have appeared disorganized according to worldly standards. On Sundays I would place boxes of bread, fruit, and vegetables along the walls of the fellowship hall at our church. I could not ignore the call of God to feed the orphans and the widows. It thrilled me to see people of all ages filling their empty sacks with food after church.

I called the ministry "The Widow's Mite," after the story in the Bible in which a widow gives her last coin as an offering. Jesus commends her for giving all she had. In God's eyes, the amount of her gift was enormous and surpassed the gifts of the religious leaders who, in the world's view, gave more.

I began to hear stories about people who found one-hundred-dollar bills stashed among the potatoes. Someone else had caught the vision of blessing others and chose to do it in a unique way by hiding money among the food. When no one was around I'd dig in the potatoes hoping to find money. To my dismay, I never did.

Once, a man who spoke at our church in an effort to raise money for missions told the pastor that he had spotted a woman in the congregation who could probably pay for every need his ministry had. I laughed when I heard this story, because he was talking about me. In reality, I barely had enough money to put gas in my car. I knew what it was like to look like a million but not have a penny.

It never crossed my mind to stop what I was doing and find other work. I knew I was doing what God wanted me to do. I had no choice but to obey. Mike helped out with the utility bills from his job as a groundskeeper. Howard began painting addresses on street curbs for my gas money, and I continued to buy and sell antiques and jewelry on the side, but soon not even that was enough.

As word of The Widow's Mite ministry began to spread, people seemed to come out of the woodwork for food. What had started out as a few boxes of fruit and vegetables sitting on a folding table had now expanded to several tables winding around the wall.

People were coming in off the street. To have seventy-five or eighty families come on Tuesdays and Sundays for food and clothing was not uncommon. Now and then someone would wander off-track and wind up in the church offices, around the building, and into the sanctuary. The church staff had a problem with strangers meandering through the building, and I didn't blame them. When someone broke through the church ceiling and stole valuable components of the sound system, more than a few eyebrows were raised.

The dream came at a time when I needed guidance and insight into what God was doing through me. I've always been a person who dreams, and I believe God speaks to me in this way. Unlike dreams I've had in the past, though, this one kept recurring and always left me in search of its full meaning.

In the dream I am pregnant and a horrible fear comes over me. *Oh, no. I don't have a husband for this baby! What will people think?* I am frightened and confused at my condition, but there is no turning back the clock. Pain shoots through my body as the labor progresses. The pain becomes excruciating, and I am covered in sweat. The final push takes every ounce of strength and determination I can give.

I am in a state of shock when a little girl pops out of me. She is not a baby; she is old enough to walk and talk. People gather around me. I hear their soothing voices as they "ooh" and "ahh" over the beautiful little girl. The girl stands to her feet and takes a wobbly step, like a fawn first learning to walk. Her next step is as unsteady as the first one. My heart sinks when I realize one leg is paralyzed.

Moans and disapproving sighs sweep over the growing throng of onlookers who have come to see what the commotion is about. I think, *Oh, no. Not only am I not married, but also she is flawed!* I run as fast as I can to the throne of God. I throw up my arms. "What am I supposed to do? No one will love her!"

God speaks. "Tell the crowd that it is OK, because she can still walk."

I race back to where the little girl stands and push my way through the crowd. I shout at the top of my lungs, "God says that she is OK! She can still walk!"

The crowd breaks out in cheers and applause. The little girl was OK; God had said so.

Next, I trace my hand along the girl's face and pull back her bangs. To my horror, I discover a third eye in the center of her forehead. Once again the people in the crowd shake their heads side to side in a disapproving way. Frightened and confused, I run back to God and beg Him to tell me what I should do. God speaks a second time: "It's OK. If you brush her bangs down, no one will even notice." I am so relieved.

When I tell the people what God said, the groaning stops. Suddenly, the little girl is perfect again, because God said she was. And then it dawns on me that this precious little girl has no name, and I am ashamed because I don't know who the father is. I go to God a third time. "What should I name her?" I plead.

"Name her Miriam," answers God.

The dream ended as the morning sun shone brilliantly through my bedroom window. I looked around, half expecting to see the little girl with three eyes lying beside me. The dream, the pregnancy, the crowd, and the little girl all seemed so real.

I pondered over the strange dream until one day I told Larie about it. I knew she had read several books on spiritual dreams and hoped she could help me interpret what God was telling me. Without leaving out a single detail, I told her about the dream.

God was faithful to give her an interpretation. I listened intently to what God was saying through my friend. "The little girl is a symbol of the food ministry. And it is also who you are. You birthed the food ministry without knowing who the father was. Although she was crippled, people received her because

God said she was OK. In the same way, you will be received by people who have abandoned and rejected you," she explained.

"But what about the third eye?" I asked.

"It is the eye of discernment. It is an eye that can see all around and discern the enemy. It is a prophetic eye. Just as Miriam was a prophetess in the Bible and a leader among women, this little girl, this food ministry, has been spiritually birthed from God. The people need to be aware that God began this ministry. And the imperfections others see will not be significant, because God said it was good," she answered.

"Why didn't people accept her when they saw her flaws?" I asked.

Larie replied, "It's easy to become a victim of our humanity. To the people the little girl represented weakness and imperfection. People don't like things that appear distorted or flawed. That is why it was so important for God to put His stamp of approval on this ministry."

I agreed. As long as God said it was OK, nothing else mattered. I held on to this word as the ministry began to grow. I was spending almost every waking hour picking up food and leaving it in the fellowship hall for people to come and take.

After two years of garage sales, newspaper dealing, and liquidation, I was running out of stuff to sell. I had my clothes, my house, my furniture, and a couple of pieces of jewelry, but almost everything else was gone. I could no longer support the ministry and myself.

It had been an unusually tiring workday. I remember thinking, *Lord, I don't know what else to sell.* And I began to cry. Of course, the devil seized the opportunity and told me how stupid I had been to have sold everything and make my family suffer. This is how the devil works. He gets you when you're tired, and I was *very* tired.

I put a stop to the enemy's voice and cried out to God. In His mercy, the Lord instructed me to call a meeting with the church elders and tell them my need. I laughed at this. "Who, *me*? You want *me* to call a meeting with the elders?" God answered, "Yes."

I trembled with fear as I made the call to set up the appointment. There were probably questions within the church about my role in The Widow's Mite ministry. Some people may have seen me as a Jezebel, a controlling and manipulating woman seeking a position of authority in the church. Possibly others saw me as a Miriam, a determined and wise leader.

But very few churches even allowed women to function in any type of ministry outside of the nursery, children's and women's ministries. If a man had headed up the food ministry, without question he would have been considered an asset. But a woman? I would be considered a "constant dripping on a rainy day," to quote Proverbs 27:15. The church had only recently been established, and here comes this woman proposing the escalation of a ministry that wasn't even in the blueprint. Our church had a music ministry, counseling, men's, women's, missions, singles, youth and children's ministries, but this? This was something that gave out and didn't bring in, and it was growing fast.

The voice of speculation rambled in my head. *Men are supposed to oversee the work in the church. If we create a ministry under her, who's going to run it when she's gone? What will happen if she marries?* The more I thought about the meeting, the more uptight I became. Soon, though, God's grace gave me a spirit of laughter that drove out all fear. I laughed and laughed. On the one hand, I was scared to death about this meeting, but God had birthed this ministry through me, and I figured He must know what He's doing. It may look illegitimate at this point, but as in the dream, the child was alive and kicking.

The meeting convened, and I told Pastor Doug and the elders what God had told me. I told them the ministry had been hard on my own children and family. My brother, Don, had made my house payments for two years, and my children had made great sacrifices so I could do this work. I felt the Lord had told me to reveal my needs to them. They asked how much money I needed to supplement my income to continue the ministry. I gave them the dollar figure. No one even blinked. It was a done deal.

The validation of me as a woman in ministry that resulted from this meeting changed my whole impression of our male-dominated staff. These were truly men of God, led by the Spirit, who were open to any leader God was raising up, male or female. I smiled at Pastor Doug. "I want you to know you are involved with this baby now," I said. He smiled back as he placed his hand on my head and said a prayer of thanksgiving and blessing for the ministry that had been birthed.

The other men looked bewildered. But Pastor Doug knew what I meant. He was the man God had chosen to pray over me when the food ministry was conceived in my heart in the dumpster on Father's Day, and now he was here to honor and bless it.

I have thought about that dream many times, and I've never questioned its validity. Almighty God, who is so big and awesome, cared enough to birth a glorious ministry to reach lost and hurting people. In spite of its flaws and imperfections, this work was operating in the natural and spiritual realms to bring about God's purposes in our city, in our church, and in our hearts. Just like those boxes of fruit and vegetables, so many people around us had been discarded, because they were considered flawed by society's standards. But those people were the heartbeat of God's work.

Chapter Eighteen

Foolish Things

My knees were skinned and bleeding as I lay under a mountain of day-old bread. My pride had taken a worse fall than my food cart when I misjudged the distance to the curb, and I landed on my bottom. I felt ridiculous buried in bread up to my elbows. With my face flushed and my self-esteem at zero, I muttered a sacriligious prayer hoping that no one had seen me fall like a fool. It was at that moment that God chose to speak to me.

Some say life begins at forty, and I believe it. My life totally changed the year I turned forty, also the year the food ministry began. My weekly trips to pick up food and haul it back to the church built muscles in my arms and legs. I shed the ten pounds I had needed to lose anyway. I began to look and feel better than I had in years.

What was known as The Widow's Mite was now called The Care Ministry. Restoration Church became the spiritual covering for the growing ministry. I wasn't a staff member, but I was in frequent contact with the staff as they came and went from the church building where my stockpile of food had found a home. This opened a door to relationships with the church secretaries who met my very deep need for fellowship. I enjoyed bagging doughnuts for distribution while gabbing about this or that. If they had extra time and things at the office were slow, they never failed to offer to help. I grew to love and cherish the friendships I was making over piles of scrumptious doughnuts.

Once when my back was aching so badly, I mustered up the courage to ask the secretaries to pray for me. I had been sleeping on the floor with a heating pad on my back at night. I had already worn out two heating pads. I was trying to avoid muscle relaxers at any cost, because they made me sluggish and drowsy.

I lifted the back of my shirt to show them where the cords from the heating pads had burned my skin. I broke into tears. "No one will ever marry me because my back is so scarred," I sobbed.

I'm sure they tried not to look shocked, but I could read their pained faces. My back looked horrible. One of the secretaries sat up straight and declared, "God can heal your back, Jackie. So in the name of Jesus I say that you are healed. Now stop using that heating pad!"

My back pain disappeared. I'd lived with back problems since I fell off the clothesline as a little girl—and especially after the car wreck, I never dreamed that I could live without pain. Now I was healed!

A few months later I was hauling a load of bread into the church. It was a muggy summer day. Sweat dripped from my forehead. My feet hurt. I looked up to see the church van loaded with the staff heading off for lunch. They smiled and waved at me from the tinted windows. I smiled and waved back, but a surge of humiliation and shame went through my body. All I could think about was how foolish and alone I felt standing in the parking lot unloading day-old bread. I wanted to be in that van. I wanted to feel as if I belonged. I thought, *Why don't they ask me to go out with them? I'm hungry too!*

I was only five years old, but I insisted on going to school like my older brother and sisters. I was a big girl. I stepped into the overcrowded first grade room and stared at the other children. The teacher walked toward me and asked, "Why Jackie, what are you doing here? Where in the world are we going to put you?" She propped her hands on her hips and looked upward. "I guess we'll just have to hang you from the ceiling!"

I froze. All I could think about were the hog corpses dangling from the ceiling in the slaughterhouse while the meat cured. I imagined myself hanging from the ceiling above the heads of the other children. To my relief Mrs. Baker found room for me to sit in the back of the crowded room. Maybe that's why I never felt like I belonged in the classroom. I was shy and withdrawn the whole year. First grade was a lonely experience.

All these years later, I still felt alone. The loaded van was a reminder that once again there was no room for a girl named Jackie. As I wallowed in self-pity, a voice spoke to me, *This is stupid! Do you know how stupid you look out here in the heat of the summer, hauling old bread around like a bag lady?*

I shook the voice away and began to push the grocery cart of bread up a narrow ramp onto the sidewalk. To my dismay, I misjudged the distance between the cart and the curb, and the next thing I knew I was on my rear covered in loaves of day-old bread. It was more than I could take, and I began to sob uncontrollably.

Through blurry eyes I watched the vanload of church staff members turning onto the busy street on their way to what I imagined would be a satisfying meal, accompanied by laughter and fellowship. I prayed to God that no one in the van had seen me fall.

I sat on the sidewalk with my knees skinned and found comfort in self-pity. The voice came again, *You see, nobody cares about what you're doing!*

I remembered the promise the Lord gave to me when I first began the food ministry from the dumpster. God told me that He was going to use the foolish things to confound the wise. It was then that the Lord spoke to me. He said, *Jackie, I told you that I was going to use the foolishness of the food ministry.*

"I don't understand what You're talking about, Lord," I pleaded.

God answered, *I'm going to use you, Jackie. You are the food ministry.*

A sense of purpose and destiny encompassed me as I sat knee-deep in a pile of bread. I stood up, brushed myself off, and finished the task at hand, which was to get the food inside the building. It was a settled issue. This was God's ministry, and He was going to use me to do His work.

The fire started mysteriously. It gutted a large portion of the shopping center where the church met. Workers were immediately called to tear down walls and build new ones. A section of the building that was once an abandoned bowling alley was remodeled to be used as the sanctuary. Restoration could now accommodate the large number of people attending the services.

The day of the fire I pulled into the church parking lot with my load of bread. I was shocked to see fire trucks and hoses in front of the building. Smoke billowed from the roof. Sirens sounded. It was a mental blow to see my church on fire. I was in shock like everyone else, and all I could think was, *Where in the world am I going to put the bread?*

Firefighters fought to contain the fire as I rescued tables from a section of the building that suffered only smoke damage. I set up my bread stand on the sidewalk, just as a child sets up a lemonade stand. And the people came.

After the debris was cleaned up, the entire building received a facelift, with a fresh coat of paint and new carpet. A large area was assigned to house the expanding food ministry. "The Father's Heart With a Mother's Touch" became the theme behind the ministry. I was given the title of care pastor by our church elders and was added to the church staff. I was free to pursue full-time what God had birthed in my heart when I was a small child sitting at those late-night revival meetings as Sister Saxton ministered hope to the lost.

After the debris was cleaned up, I sat in the vacant room designated for The Care Ministry. The bare floors and the barren walls swallowed me. "God, where on earth do I begin? This room is too big," I prayed.

Little by little, God began to create a vision in my heart. A talented artist painted a mural of Jesus sitting alone in the Garden of Gethsemane. A woman handed me a check for ten thousand dollars to buy a commercial freezer to hold perishable goods like meat and pizzas. Volunteers pitched in to build shelves and organize the space I had been given. I had my own office. I even had my own bathroom!

Blessings kept coming my way. Driving to work one day I spotted some countertops in the parking lot of a restaurant. The building was apparently being remodeled, and I wasn't about to let a good deal like that pass me by. I asked to speak to the restaurant manager. With the boldness of a lion, I explained the purpose of The Care Ministry. I came right out and asked if he would donate the countertops. He scratched his head as if he had never given thought to what was to become of them. With a handshake—and my promise to remove the countertops from the parking lot—we sealed the deal. I wanted to shout.

I opened the doors to The Care Ministry five days a week for food distribution. The many volunteers who joined me gave unselfishly of their time and talents. We worked night and day together, sometimes rubbing shoulders, learning to resolve personality clashes and growing to love one another more each day.

The Bible says, "Man does not live on bread alone, but on every word that comes from the mouth of God" (Matt. 4:4). I knew that deep inside, the people we served were hungry to know God. One of the reasons they came was to be a part of His church, a church that would care about their problems, feed and clothe them, and shepherd their souls. The Care Ministry was *their* church.

It was always my intention to combine the ministry of the Word with the food distribution. We encouraged people to attend a short devotional service before they received their food. In the beginning, I asked students at Emmaus Road Ministry School, which was then affiliated with Restoration Church, to preach the services while I picked up the food. Later, others began to pick up the food for me, and I preached on a regular basis. At first, only a few came to hear the sermons. Then more and more came. Not everyone who received food heard the sermons, but if people happened to be standing around outside, waiting, smoking a cigarette, I would invite them in. They'd be too shocked to say no. Many people came into church this way. And you know what? Soon a lot of them began to come on their own, without my asking them.

I called this informal church service "Happy Hour" as a reminder of my own spiritual journey, and I posted a sign listing the hours of operation. It was a "Happy Hour" sign that had first drawn me back into the church fold when I was so desperately searching for a better life for my children and me. I trusted that the friendly slogan would do the same for other people in search of a place of joy and rest.

"Happy Hour" was a safe place for people who readily came to sing praise songs, listen to a brief sermon, and give what little they had as the offering bucket was passed. My childhood dream came to fruition whenever I preached what God had put on my heart that day. Sometimes I invited people to share their testimonies.

What amazed me most was how people would faithfully drop coins and dollar bills into the offering bucket week after week. I believe God was training them in the basic principle of sowing and reaping. "Give and it shall be given"—what better way to learn the dynamics of God's kingdom and how it operates?

As people passed through the food line, I tried to hug and touch each and every one. Sometimes I'd feel them pull back and get as stiff as a poker. They didn't know how to hug. Many were not used to being touched at all. Some people, particularly men, would be embarrassed by the gesture. Maybe they feared it would tarnish their tough-guy image. Part of the beauty of The Care Ministry service was in offering such men the opportunity to lower their guard and allow the love of God to soften their hearts.

I have come to realize that God's plans far exceed our human comprehension. He uses ordinary people like you and me to bring about what would be impossible to do on our own. God has always chosen the weak and foolish things to confound the wise of this world. I'm living proof of that.

Chapter Nineteen

The Shadow of Death

*It was a mother's worst nightmare. I saw my son
lying in the driveway next to his pickup. The gun rested
on his lifeless body. I fell to the ground and cradled
Mike as a mother cradles her newborn. I told him how
much I loved him and how badly I wanted him back. As
the paramedics pulled the sheet over his head and
loaded his body into the ambulance, I let the rush of
tears flow.*

It had been an unbearably painful and exhausting
delivery. Finally, after thirty-six hours of grueling labor
my baby boy was born. It was June 18, 1962. The doctor
held him upside down by his tiny, wrinkled ankles and
slapped his bottom with his free hand.

I watched helplessly as my baby dangled like a rag
doll, not making a sound. The doctor spanked him again
and again, to no avail. I gasped for air, wanting to breathe
for my son, but this was his battle. I hoped and prayed that
he would instinctively know to fight for survival.

Minutes later a faint whimper broke the deathly silence, and he began to cry. Tears of joy streamed down my cheeks. My baby was going to live.

The next day the nurse brought him into my hospital room for his mid-morning feeding, and he began to cry. I shifted his little body to make him more comfortable, but his cries grew louder. Within seconds his cry turned into a blood-curdling scream until there was no sound or breath coming out of him at all. His face turned a deep shade of red.

"Help! Somebody help me!" I yelled at the top of my lungs.

The nurse ran into the room just as my son began to turn blue. I was frantic. "He's not breathing! He's not breathing!" I screamed. I shoved him toward the nurse as I yelled for her to help him breathe. I watched in horror as his face now started to turn bluish purple.

The next hours and days of his life were a nightmarish blur. I recall the doctors placing a long tube into his lungs to give him oxygen and rushing him by ambulance to another hospital that was better equipped to handle emergencies. This was to be the beginning of a long journey of tragedies and triumphs in my son's life.

Every parent dreams of having a healthy child with ten fingers and ten toes, seeing eyes, hearing ears. After his initial brush with death, Mike appeared to be a healthy, happy baby, always smiling. He had the clearest sky-blue eyes and beautiful curly blond hair.

The day he finally took his first steps I almost shot through the roof with ecstasy! I was in the Laundromat finishing up a load of clothes when he tottered toward me.

My throat clogged with a shout of joy that erupted as he tumbled to the floor a few steps later. I jumped. I clapped. I cheered in spite of the stares from other people.

At three years old, Mike was constantly tripping over his own feet whenever he tried to run or walk too fast. His knees and elbows were covered with bruises from the daily spills and falls. I took Mike to the Texas Scottish Rite Hospital for Children in Dallas.

Mike was diagnosed with cerebral palsy. The medical staff attributed his condition to the loss of oxygen as he made a dangerously slow descent down the birth canal during the perilous moments preceding his birth. The doctor's straightforward explanation of Mike's condition was plain and clear; he would live with this condition the rest of his life.

Clunky braces were strapped on to both legs to correct his inability to walk. It saddened me to watch him trying to manage those stiff metal rods, moving them back and forth in an effort to walk without falling down.

Mike was like the lead character in the movie *Forrest Gump*. As I watched the movie years later, I sat in the theater with a big box of popcorn and cried my eyes out. The character reminded me of my little Mike running clumsily across the lawn in those awkward leg braces, trying his best to keep up with the other children.

Throughout his school years Mike attended special-education classes. He was so proud of his report cards; he always made an A in academics and an A-plus in conduct. He was the nicest person I've ever met.

One day when the kids were riding their bikes home from school, a bully approached Mike and Charlsey and pushed Mike off his bike. I had taught my children to never start a fight but also to never run from one. Charlsey retaliated with her fist. As always, Charlsey defended her older brother.

As the fight escalated, Mike did something totally out of character. He got off the ground, took off his belt, and began whipping the bully. The boy ended up jumping on his bike and riding away as fast as he could go. Up until that time Mike had never stood up for himself. I was proud of him and saw this event as a courageous landmark that would supply him with the confidence to face other hardships in life.

On his graduation day I was as proud as any mother could be as I watched my son walk across the stage to receive his high school diploma. He wore his favorite white suit with his baby-blue shirt, the one that brought out the blue in his eyes. As he walked proudly across the gymnasium stage in his cap and gown, I exploded with pride. Mike had beaten the odds. He could read at only an elementary level, but he had worked tirelessly in special classes learning how to survive in a world where handicaps were too often a deterrent to success.

Mike was labeled as "educatable," meaning that he could be taught certain things—like how to fill out an application, manage small amounts of money, and drive a car. He could read street signs, but not a map. Mike got his driver's license by taking the written test orally.

After graduation he first worked at McDonald's and later as a groundskeeper at an apartment complex. Every day he meticulously prepared for his job. He kept his bedroom immaculate and his maintenance uniform ironed to perfection. He carefully combed every hair into place and topped off his daily preparations with a generous splash of cologne. If I hadn't known better, I would have thought my son worked at some high-paying job as an executive.

Mike was a superb employee. He was never late for work and showed respect toward his boss. At home he was just as respectful and polite. The only time Mike defied me was when I asked him to give up chewing tobacco. Well, he didn't take too kindly to my request and told me so. We came to a mutual agreement; his habit had to stay out of the house and out of my sight.

I could always depend on Mike to lend me any spare cash he had. Unfortunately, he did this for anyone else who asked him for money, even strangers. One time, I discovered that his bank account was overdrawn. "Where did your money go?" I asked.

Mike shrugged his shoulders and gave a worried look. It dawned on me that since he couldn't keep any type of financial records, he had no way of knowing if he wrote a bad check. After some investigation, I found several checks written to a single mother who lived in the apartments where he worked. He had paid her rent numerous times but somehow assumed the money was still in the bank.

Mike was also my prayer partner. Every night he would go outside, sit in his chair under the big oak tree in front, and pray for our family. He had a special call on his life for evangelism. He didn't feel the confidence to preach, but he would hand out tracts. Almost every weekend he'd stuff his briefcase full of tracts that described how to become a Christian. I'd drop him off at a mall near our home where he spent hours handing tracts to anyone who would take one. He was never ashamed of being a witness for the Lord.

One day he phoned me from the mall, his voice full of excitement. It took a few moments for me to piece the story together. Apparently a teenage boy had read one of the tracts and wanted to become a Christian right then and there. Well, Mike panicked because he couldn't read and didn't know exactly what to tell this boy. It just so happened that a man sitting on a bench nearby had witnessed the whole incident and volunteered to lead this kid to the Lord. Mike watched excitedly as the stranger carefully read the tract to this young man and led him in a prayer to give his heart to Jesus.

Years later I was listening to a preacher give his testimony. He explained how he had given his heart to Jesus simply because someone had the courage to hand him a Christian tract at the mall. He described how his life had changed after that encounter. I closed my eyes and visualized Mike as God's faithful servant sowing seeds into ready and willing hearts. I like to think it was Mike who had a hand in saving this man's soul.

After the downfall of several religious leaders in the mid-1980s, Mike began to sink into a depression. Like so many others, he felt confused and disillusioned by the men he had watched on television, men he had trusted. He stopped handing out tracts.

When I asked him what was wrong, he lowered his eyes and said sadly, "Mom, nobody wants to hear about Jesus. They don't want to know what the Bible says. Nobody cares." He was becoming withdrawn, and this really concerned me.

In the past, few things had thrilled Mike more than the weekend fishing trips he'd take with my father. I'd ask, "What did you and Granddad talk about?" He'd shrug his shoulders.

"We talk about Jesus and what heaven is like, stuff like that," he would answer.

But my father became sick, and they weren't able to go fishing anymore. Mike began to spend his time tuning up his pickup truck. He'd spend hours with his head under the hood, checking the oil, listening to the engine. But he could never hide the loneliness he felt. He needed a friend.

One day I looked out the window and noticed a man talking to Mike as he worked on his truck. I could tell this man was showing an interest in whatever my son was telling him and seemed to be offering some tips of his own. He walked by every day at the same time in the early evening and stopped whenever Mike was out front. I saw them talk and laugh. It thrilled me to see my son relating to someone in this way. This man would stop and talk for only a few minutes, but that was just enough to encourage Mike and brighten his day.

Mike liked routine and didn't handle change very well. So when his boss transferred him to another apartment complex in a different section of town, his life was disrupted. For one thing, since Mike couldn't read a map he had to work hard to memorize the new route to and from work. The roads were unfamiliar to him, and he had to say good-bye to familiar faces that had greeted him at work each day and made him feel secure.

To complicate matters, there had been an unseasonable amount of rainfall and many roads were closed due to flooding. One evening I watched helplessly as Mike walked through the front door drenched and shaking. He was hours late. When I asked him what had happened, he bit his lower lip to keep back the tears. He stuttered,

"The...the...the streets had water on them, Mom. I...I...got lost 'cause I didn't know how to get home. I...I...was scared." It was times like this I questioned the Lord and asked, "Why do You allow innocent people to go through such hard trials?" But He doesn't ask us to go through anything that He hasn't gone through Himself.

I held my grown son in my arms and cried with him. There were many more tears to come. For starters, his new manager was a cruel woman who treated Mike disrespectfully. She called him an idiot and stupid, among other things. I wasn't aware of her behavior at the time; if I had known, I would have immediately intervened.

I also learned that other groundsworkers taunted him when he didn't comprehend their dirty jokes. Mike had never engaged in sex, much less even kissed a girl. The jabs and sneers hurt him deeply, although he didn't understand exactly why they were laughing. He only knew they were laughing at him.

Around this time he began to feel an attraction toward a woman at work. This encouraged me, because I knew he was capable of a romantic relationship with a woman. Mike would have made a wonderful husband. He was faithful and kind. Most important, Mike could love. For a brief time he seemed to snap out of his depression, and then, as quickly as it had left, the depression returned, taking him into a deeper level of despair and loneliness.

Meanwhile, in October of 1989 my attention to Mike and his needs was suddenly diverted in another direction entirely. I returned home after working at The Care Ministry all day and checked my answering machine. The Colleyville police department had called: Howard had been hit by a car and had been taken to the hospital.

Terrified and shaking, I rushed to the hospital and found Howard, who was fifteen at the time, in the emergency room in excruciating pain. He was hit by a car while riding his moped not ten feet from the trash bin where he had found that first bunch of grapes. One of his legs was broken and in traction; Howard had to be sedated with morphine until the leg could be set.

Howard stayed in the hospital for three weeks and received several units of blood due to a stress-induced bleeding ulcer. I had no medical insurance, and the bill came to twenty-five thousand dollars. (I later worked out a pay arrangement with the hospital.)

I didn't care. I was just grateful that my son was alive. He was home by the first week in November, and now that it was clear that he was fine, I could focus on the upcoming holidays and the special holiday events at church.

I breathed a long sigh of relief.

November 16 of that year was cold and damp. Mike decided to stay home from work, which was uncharacteristic of him. With the exception of a few days when he was far too sick to work, he had never missed a day of work. He had vacation days on top of vacation days waiting to be used. But on this particular day, Mike told me he wanted to stay home. The evening before, he had brought his tools home from work, which was something he had never done before. I figured he needed to clean them or something. If nothing else, I was relieved that he was taking a day off.

That evening I came home after working at the food ministry and zapped a meal in the microwave before rushing out again to rehearse for a Thanksgiving program at our church. Mike said he wasn't hungry, which was typical. He was thin from all the miles he walked doing lawn care, and food was never a concern for him. I shoved a bite of food in my mouth. Mike sat next to me.

I finished chewing. "I'm glad you took the day off. What did you do?" I asked.

"Oh, I went fishing. I didn't catch anything, really. Only some little ones, but I had a fun time," he answered.

I smiled at him. He looked good. He looked more rested and relaxed than I'd seen him in months. "I'm so glad you had a good time," I said. "I'm going to music practice tonight at church. Howard's going to a friend's house. If you get hungry why don't you go over to Mother and Daddy's for supper? They'd love to see you."

And so he did.

But sometime after supper and before choir practice ended, Mike took his life. I had no idea that our dinnertime conversation was to be our last. It would be the last time I would look into his blue eyes, hear his sweet voice, feel his presence, smell his hair, or touch his skin. The pain was too much to bear.

Chapter Twenty

Two Tickets to Paradise

As the sun peeked over the horizon, reality set in. I had spent the night identifying my son's body, contacting relatives and close friends, and answering routine questions posed by the police officer in charge. General procedure, they called it. It was the darkest night of my life.

Mike had owned the shotgun for some time. It was one of those long shotguns used for hunting. Charlsey's husband had asked him to go hunting several times, but the trip never panned out. Mike didn't know beans about how to shoot a gun.

I spotted Mike's pickup in the back part of the driveway, so I knew he was home. When I set foot in the house, a chill went through my bones. It felt empty. I immediately knew something was wrong, terribly wrong. I rushed to Howard's room. He and a friend were listening to the radio and talking.

"Where's Mike?" I asked, trying to hide my fear.

"He's probably in the backyard working on his truck," answered Howard.

I called out the back door. "Mike! Mike! Are you back here? Answer me!" I shouted.

No answer.

I walked outside. The floodlight was on in the backyard. I saw his body. He was lying flat on his back a few feet from the bed of the truck with his arms and legs outstretched. His eyes and mouth were closed as he lay undisturbed on the ground.

There was nothing weird or ugly about the way he looked. My first thought was, *Surely he isn't sleeping out here!*

Then I saw the gun. It was pointed toward him. "Oh God! No! No! No!" One of my first thoughts was, *God, do You want me to call him back from the dead?* He said, "No, he's with Me." My arms and legs were trembling as I leaned over his still body. I knelt down and kissed his forehead as a mother does when saying goodnight to her sleeping child.

Through broken sobs I spoke to my son. "Mikey, you are the most wonderful son a mother could ever have. I wouldn't have changed you for anything. You are the most wonderful boy in the world. I love you, Mike. I love you. I love you..." My words trailed off in a weary whisper. I cherish those moments I spent alone with my son.

The ambulance and police arrived, and neighbors stood on their front lawns watching curiously as the sirens screamed and the lights lit up the quiet suburban street. I considered it to be a gift from God that his body was so perfect. When the coroners arrived they found one spot of blood under his jacket. The size of the blast should have blown a hole in him.

Later I read the coroner's report, indicating that a single bullet made a clean, swift shot, hitting several vital organs. This accounted for the small amount of blood on his body. The report also said he died instantly, which is why there was no sign of pain or trauma to his body. By all appearances, Mike's death was a suicide.

The police, on the other hand, didn't consider this to be an open-and-shut case. There was no suicide note, although that is not unusual. I explained to the police that my son couldn't read, much less express himself in a suicide note.

The detectives gathered their information on that terrible night and considered the case open, but I knew in my heart that Mike had taken his life. In retrospect, all the warning signs were there. He had brought his tools home, had not gone to work, and had made his peace with himself and the world. I knew him well enough to know he viewed death not as a way out but as a way to be with God. And he was ready to go. Eventually, his death was ruled a suicide.

I know it would have been more acceptable to society if Mike had died in an automobile accident. I've gone over that day a million times in my mind. I've asked myself a thousand times what I could have done differently.

If I had known then what I know now about depression, I would have taken Mike to a doctor and gotten him on antidepressants. Even though depression afflicts hundreds of thousands of people a year, talking about it is still taboo in most churches. We tend to think people are unspiritual if they can't snap out of it—so we don't offer the right kind of help. As a result, depression often lingers and increases in intensity.

Mike fit into one statistic of depression very neatly. While women who suffer from depression attempt suicide at least as often as men do, it's the men who are more often "successful" in their attempts.

God can give life through doctors and antidepressant drugs, just as He can through divine healing. It took me years to let go of the guilt and shame I felt over my blindness to Mike's illness. I berated myself for not taking him to a doctor and getting him on medication to elevate his mood. I finally had to let go of the "What ifs?" and "I should haves" in order to come to terms with my son's premature death, not just for my family's sake, but for my own healing.

Without question, when a child dies a part of the parent dies also. There will always be an empty place in my heart, a longing and aching that only Mike can fill. Until we are reunited in heaven, this painful place will stay in the hidden corridors of my heart. But there are also many happy places, and there is life in me that no person or thing can quench. It is the life that flows from my relationship with a living God who allows me to relate to my living children, family, friends, and church. It is the part of me that lives on in spite of hardship, tragedy, and despair.

The funeral was held at Restoration Church and was officiated by Pastor Doug and Mike's pastors at Colleyville Assembly of God. The love and support shown by my church family overwhelmed me. Mike was dressed in his favorite white suit with the blue shirt, and although his eyes were closed, I could still imagine how blue they were.

The tiny faded red and lavender specks on his suit brought a smile to my face. I remembered the times he wore that suit to communion services. His hand would shake, and he never failed to spill more wine on his clothes than he was able to drink. He'd take his suit off after church, and it would go to the cleaners once again. It's amazing he was able to wear that suit as long as he did. Once he had reached a certain height, Mike's weight never fluctuated more than a few pounds; I think he could have worn that suit for another twenty years had he lived.

I chose to make the funeral a celebration of Mike's life rather than a mourning of his death. There would be many days to come that I would cry by his bed, smell his clothes, trace my hand over his tools and his fishing gear, and whisper his name.

Before leaving the house for the church, I told Charlsey that I wished I had known the name of the man who stopped and talked to Mike out by the pickup every day. I had no way of telling him about the funeral service, and I regretted that. But the service was an uplifting time of praise and worship, even though so many in my family were overcome with grief. Charlsey and Mike were almost like twins growing up. She even chose to go with Mike to Trinity High School, which was outside the district. At that last viewing of her brother, she was overcome with grief and fainted at the casket.

At the end of the viewing line I looked up, and standing between the casket and me was Mike's friend. I threw my arms around him and broke into tears of joy.

"You're here! You're here!" I cried. I turned to everyone and exclaimed, "This is Mike's friend!"

After the funeral I never saw that man again. Who knows? He may have been an angel assigned to Mike. Or perhaps he was an ordinary person who took the time to listen and be a friend to my son. I have never since underestimated the power of a simple gesture of friendship.

Just when I was finally able to put so much of the grief behind me, the past came back to haunt me. Four years after Mike's death, an attractive, middle-aged blonde walked into my office and told me a heartbreaking story. "I worked with Mike," she said nervously.

I immediately motioned for her to come in and sit down. I looked at the child-sized metal shoe brace balanced against my office window. I kept it there not only as a tribute to my son's life but as a reminder of all the walking wounded who fill the streets and sidewalks each day, in need of hope and a friend. The tattered brown shoe that connected to the brace rested on the window as a streak of sunlight framed the moment.

"I'm here to tell you something I feel you must know about some of the things Mike went through before he..." she paused as if it pained her to say the word "died."

I locked the door. "Tell me, please," I said.

Tears coursed freely from my eyes, and my heart shattered as she told me about the horrible, cruel treatment Mike had endured over the last few months of his life. The apartment manager openly teased Mike in front of everyone. It was her idea to have him dress like a werewolf at the staff Halloween party. One week after the funeral, the apartment manager sent me a picture of Mike wearing the werewolf mask. I almost died of fright. That had to be the cruelest thing a person could have done to a grieving mother.

Mike's co-worker told me she had married an attorney shortly after Mike's death, and after a year of marriage he took his own life in their home. I do not believe she came with the intent to hurt me, but the things she shared hurt me nevertheless.

The woman told me how she befriended Mike. The friendship ended as abruptly as it began, when she realized he was becoming infatuated with her. The prospect of having any type of relationship beyond friendship caused her to take drastic measures to keep Mike's feelings at bay.

She had his heart on a platter one day when he walked into her office. "I've got two tickets to paradise. Do you want to go?" he asked.

"I told him why I couldn't go and why we could no longer spend time together," she nervously explained. "I heard how he had taken his life. For years I've kept our last conversation a secret."

In seconds my sorrow dissolved into anger. Everything in me wanted to blame her. I hated this woman for the insensitive way she toyed with my son's heart. I blamed her for not coming to me sooner. I wanted to blame myself for not seeing the signs before he died. I wanted to blame God for allowing my son to take his life.

The pain bottled up inside of me was too much to bear. As soon as this woman left my office I buried my face in my hands and cried out to Jesus to give me grace to survive the heartbreak I felt after hearing this woman's story. I could only imagine the pain Mike must have felt by putting his heart on the line, only to have it rejected.

Exposed Heart

When the tears subsided I left work and headed for the nearest music store in our city. "Do you have a tape with a song called 'Two Tickets to Paradise'?" I asked.

The store employee led me to the tape. I purchased it and inserted it in the tape deck in my car. I listened to the song carefully as I pieced together what must have been Mike's last thoughts.

In that song, "paradise" referred to heaven. "Two Tickets to Paradise" was about leaving this world to go to a better place. Mike had gotten his wish.

Chapter Twenty-One

Mr. Bill's Angel

Beads of rain dotted the hospital window. I held a private vigil beside my dying friend's bed. God had not answered my prayer to heal her of the cancer that riddled her body. I longed to see a miracle happen. I wanted to see death conquered. But God had a different plan. Just before she took her last breath, I asked, "Joyce, when you get to heaven, will you tell Mike I love him?"

For a season death seemed to be a constant companion. Kimberly, a young lady who had found Jesus through The Care Ministry, was a recovering drug addict. Her love for God spilled from her soul as she danced and lifted her hands during songs of worship. She was tragically taken from us when a car struck her after she had stopped to scoop a dead animal off the road. Her compassion for animals—and for all of God's creation, for that matter—cost her her life.

My family has always been important to me, more than they'll ever know. After Mike's death we grew even closer. The uncertainty of life caused me to cherish every moment I spent with my children and their families. I was made a grandmother at the age of forty when Charlsey gave birth to my first grandson, Isaiah. Howard later blessed me with two precious granddaughters, Cierra and Alexis.

Children are not exempt from the pain their parents go through. Every divorce, every beating wasn't just about me. These hardships inflicted wounds in my children's hearts as well. With divorce so prevalent in our society, children often become the victims of bitter custody battles and bear the brunt of their parents' pain. I grieve over the scars on my children caused by years of tumultuous relationships and beatings. But while I would give anything to go back and undo the mistakes I made, the suffering my children endured while growing up has undoubtedly shaped them into the strong and determined individuals they are today.

My family never brought up my past mistakes. They only cautioned me to listen to the voice of God and walk in obedience. This was a simple lesson I had been brought up with. My parents as well as my brother and sisters and their spouses continued to be strong supporters of the work God had called me to do. In fact, they believed in me more than I did.

They weren't the least bit surprised as The Care Ministry continued to grow by leaps and bounds. People swarmed in week after week to receive food and to hear a message of hope about a loving God who cares about every single person. I never made Happy Hour a prerequisite for getting food, nor did I try to manipulate people when the offering was taken. And yet people continued to give from their pockets and their hearts.

"Give, and it will be given to you," the Bible teaches in Luke 6:38. This spiritual principle is essential to Christian maturity. The people continued to plunk nickels, dimes and quarters into the offering bucket before lining up to fill their grocery sacks with fruit, vegetables, gourmet desserts, deli-quality bread, and premium meat. Their understanding of God's principle of giving never failed to give my spirit a lift. I knew that these people were giving out of their need and that God would reward them.

With its growing crowds the ministry was catapulted to a new level of responsibility and workload. There was no way I could have kept The Care Ministry going without the help of many selfless and faithful volunteers who freely gave of their time. But soon volunteers were not enough.

The elders of our church agreed to add others to the payroll to keep The Care Ministry in operation. Ross was the first volunteer to become an employee. His strong arms and gentle spirit allowed him to minister the love of God as he gathered food from area stores and hauled it to the church for The Care Ministry. Sylvia became my second pair of ears, eyes, and hands. Her discernment and secretarial skills kept my head above water many times. Susan's administrative skills and passion for The Care Ministry enabled her to take my place as the coordinator. Her quiet demeanor and organizational skills kept the ministry afloat. And there were many others who gave of their time and energy. Without a doubt the ministry had evolved to a point where I could never have continued on my own.

As more and more people gave their hearts to Jesus, lives began to change. It dawned on me one day that I was indeed their pastor. But how was I to perform the basic functions of ministry without a minister's license? I was unable to marry the couple who had been living together and now wanted to obey God by getting married. How was I to bury loved ones without proper licensing from the state? In a nutshell, without a minister's license I was unable to marry and bury the very people who called me their pastor. The importance of a license brewed in my spirit until God made it clear to me that this was an important step I needed to take.

Determined to follow my heart, in the fall of 1991 I received my minister's license through Gospel Assemblies in Missouri. At last I was able to meet the practical as well as spiritual needs of The Care Ministry's growing congregation as an ordained minister.

By following my heart to seek a minister's license, I saw how the Lord was able to open avenues of ministry that I would not have been able to follow had I not been ordained. I'll never forget the day I received a call from the city regarding the death of a vagrant who lived most of his life on a park bench, taking handouts from strangers. No family members came forward, and the city asked me to conduct a burial service for him. Although this man was homeless, he had been a constant fixture, and people knew him as a kind, gentle man with no name. I buried him with honor and respect.

I believe this vagrant who died alone on a park bench represented the people I pastored through The Care Ministry— people who often slipped through society's cracks. These are the people, I believe, that Jesus wants to reach through us. As we sit comfortably in church each Sunday, without regard to what exists beyond those four walls, we will continue to grieve the Holy Spirit. It is God's heart to heal the brokenhearted, set the captives free, and restore their lives to His original purpose. God chooses us in spite of our flaws and weaknesses to carry out this magnificent calling through the power of the Holy Spirit.

It was customary for our family to get together on Christmas Day to share a holiday meal and exchange gifts. But Christmas of 1995 was different. My mother insisted we gather on the twenty-third of December instead of Christmas Day. My father had been feeling ill for some time, but even so that was no reason to move up our Christmas gathering by two days. But it seemed to be an OK plan, so I agreed to the change in the date.

No one else seemed to care about this breach in tradition either. What mattered was that we were all together, crowded around the dinner table with growling stomachs, ready to stuff our mouths with my mother's delicious home cooking. It was a picture-perfect event.

As my father bowed his head to say the blessing, he did something unusual. Instead of simply thanking God for the food, he spoke a prayer of blessing over each person seated around the table—children, grandchildren, and great-grandchildren. Sometimes I wonder if he somehow knew this would be our last time together.

When my mother called the following day, I was stunned at what she told me. My father had died in his sleep. It seemed surreal. We had spent his last evening alive feasting on turkey, dressing, and the works, and exchanging gifts. Nothing could have prepared me for my mother's grim news.

No! This can't be happening! my thoughts screamed.

I threw on a pair of jeans and an oversized sweat top and raced out the door. I arrived before anyone else, including the paramedics. My father lay on his bed as if asleep. He looked so peaceful. The tears fell from my eyes like flowing streams. I touched his still hand. "I love you, Daddy. I love you," I whispered between sobs.

A few months after my father's death, another death occurred in The Care Ministry. One of our faithful volunteers, Mr. Bill, collapsed to the floor while bagging groceries. He was ninety-nine, and we were all surprised Mr. Bill had lived that long, but he had the vigor of a much younger man. It was his dream to live to be one hundred, and I promised him we'd pull off the party of the century when he reached that milestone.

Death's ever-present theme in my life drove me to the brink of despair. I couldn't sit by and watch one more person die, not today anyway. I didn't care if Mr. Bill was ninety-nine or eighteen. Something inside of me said this wasn't meant to be. I dropped to the floor and began to pray.

"Call 911...we're losing Mr. Bill!" someone yelled.

Maybe everyone thought I was nuts, but I didn't care. Mr. Bill's face had turned a pale gray, his eyes had rolled back in his head, and we could find only the faintest pulse in his body. "Mr. Bill, you are not going to die," I insisted. "In the name of Jesus, I command life to come back into your body!

Suddenly, Mr. Bill sneezed lightly, and his body went totally limp. We couldn't find a pulse. A nurse once told me that it was common for a person to blow out a puff of air, burp, or sneeze when the spirit left the body. I felt as if this was happening to Mr. Bill. I had already buried a son and, more recently, my father. I wasn't ready to give up on Mr. Bill. And yet, by all accounts, he was dead.

I stroked his cold hand. "We need you, Mr. Bill. I love you...I love you," I said over and over. As the volunteers stood around the room watching they must have thought, "She's losing her mind!" Then Mr. Bill sneezed twice more. The volunteers, excited by his response, cried out, "We love you, Mr. Bill." I felt faith rise up in me. "In the name of Jesus, I command life to come back in you," I prayed.

Mr. Bill sneezed three more times and then slowly opened his eyes. He looked up at his audience. Relief swept over all of us. I felt that I had just witnessed a miracle!

Minutes later, when the paramedics arrived, Mr. Bill was sitting up sipping juice from a paper cup. They checked his vital signs, which turned out to be normal! The paramedics got ready to place him on a stretcher. "I don't need to go to the hospital," Mr. Bill informed them.

"Sir, you've been through something traumatic, and we need to check you out and make sure everything is OK," said one of the paramedics.

Mr. Bill gave them a disgusted look. "I'm ninety-nine," he muttered.

I guess his age was enough to convince them, because they left without him.

Suddenly, I was aware of my body. I was weak and lightheaded. It was as if every ounce of strength had left my body when I prayed for my friend. I fought my way to the bathroom and took a deep breath. My body shook. I wondered if this was how Jesus had felt when the woman with an issue of blood touched His garment in the midst of a huge crowd. Somehow Jesus knew He had been touched because He felt power leave His body. At that moment Jesus turned around and asked, "Who touched Me?"

Staring into the bathroom mirror I thought of the scripture found in John 14:12: "Anyone who has faith in Me...will do even greater things than these." I continued to shake from the top of my head to the bottom of my feet. *"God, is this what You meant? Do we really have the power to raise people from the dead?"* I knew I already had the answer to my question. Yes, as a child of God I had the power to do the same miracles Jesus did when He walked the earth. I, too, could raise the dead.

It was all I could do to head to the church kitchen to find something to eat. I rummaged through the refrigerator, only to find a piece of bologna. I nibbled on the slice, trying to

173

regain some strength. I was weak and at the same time strong in my spirit, knowing God had used me to bring life into someone who was dying. It was the most fun I'd ever had!

That day, death had been conquered! Faith exploded in my heart, and I began to shout praises to God. I made my way back to the room where Mr. Bill was sitting and hugged his neck.

He smiled at me. "I had a dream about you last night," he said.

"Oh, really?" I asked.

"Yes, I dreamed you were my angel."

At that moment I knew beyond a shadow of a doubt that God had worked a miracle to bring a dying man back to life. I had witnessed a miracle, and my life would never be the same.

Chapter Twenty-Two

The Cost of Ministry

It had been a long week, and I was exhausted. I couldn't wait to peel off my shoes and soak my feet in a warm tub. It was time to relax and unwind after a grueling week of packaging food and ministering to people's needs. I hopped into my van, and turned on the air-conditioning and a little music to soothe my nerves. Pulling onto the highway, I saw a young woman with her thumb raised. I knew I had no choice but to stop and pick her up.

Just as my father had once predicted, The Care Ministry was like a budding tree that kept growing new branches of ministry. God began enlarging my vision to go out and share Jesus with people who might not ever set foot in a church.

To my amazement mountains of food poured in week after week as more and more dedicated volunteers came to help. I was overwhelmed with the love and support my church family showed when an offering was taken that allowed me to buy a new, much-needed van. Several billboards in our city were donated to the ministry to reach hurting women. I hoped the billboards would catch the eye of those who needed care and wanted to escape their destructive lifestyles.

At Thanksgiving and Christmas, people seemed to come out of the woodwork to donate money to pay for baskets filled with turkey and all the trimmings. With the help of hundreds of volunteers, The Care Ministry hosted an annual Christmas party for all the families who had come for food throughout the year. Again, the people of Restoration Church filled the need by donating hundreds of new toys to be purchased, wrapped, and handed out at the party.

One particular holiday season I lived out one of my childhood fantasies. The children's pastor at our church asked me if I had ever considered dressing up like an angel for the children's ministry. While the thought had never occurred to me, I liked the idea. Even if I weren't an angel, a costume would be a tangible display of celestial life and remind others of the existence of angels. Convinced this was a good idea, I got myself all decked out in a glittery costume and welcomed the children. Heavy makeup and a sparkling halo almost convinced *me* that I was an angel.

As a child I had often thought about angels and wondered what it would be like to be one. Not that I'd ever know, but it was still fun to pretend. In reality, I had the same need for friendship and the love of Jesus as the people who came year after year to our Christmas party. The costume was merely a reminder that angels really do exist and that God uses them to remind us of His presence in our everyday lives, to give us hope.

The children responded with excitement, and I decided to carry the idea over to The Care Ministry's annual Christmas party. I remember taking a deep breath as I stared at the tall Christmas tree sparkling with tinsel, bows, and hundreds of flickering white lights. Finger foods swallowed the entire table;

it was hard to imagine that it would actually all be eaten. Hundreds of new toys wrapped in colorful packages were placed in the hands of all of the children who had come to The Care Ministry for food during the year. This was a party only God could pull off!

And pull it off He did.

Children who would normally receive hand-me-down gifts or nothing at all stared in wide-eyed wonder at the Christmas miracle happening before their eyes. And they knew Jesus was the reason for the spectacular event. Squeals of delight filled the fellowship hall as wrapping paper flew into the air in colorful shreds, revealing a new, quality toy picked especially for the specific gender and age groups. The room resounded with Christmas joy. The angel costume added flair to an already exciting evening.

It had been a long week. I was really tired. I had been on my feet about fourteen hours a day. It was all I could do to keep my eyes open. Finally, I dropped what I was doing and said, "Forget it. I've got to go home and get some rest." As I climbed into the van, I envisioned the pleasure I'd feel as I unplugged the phone and kicked off my shoes.

Pulling onto the freeway I noticed a woman walking alongside the road with her thumb raised. My first thought was, *Lord, I hope she will be OK. I hope she gets a ride. Lord, please help that woman.* I had gone maybe a quarter of a mile down the road when I heard His still, small voice inside me. It was the same voice I had heard so many times before.

"You have to go back," He whispered.

I pulled off on the shoulder and backed up to where she was, while carefully trying to stay out of the way of oncoming cars. I took off my diamond ring and placed it in a small compartment inside the van.

I weighed my decision, knowing full well it was not smart for a woman alone to pick up a hitchhiker. I considered the very real possibility that I could lose my life. But after all, how could I go past her with a sign on the van that read "Ministry to Hurting Women"? I waved to her to hop in. She climbed in, and for some reason I assumed she was going a short distance.

"So, where are you going?" I asked.

"I need a ride to a friend's apartment," she answered. She looked tired but grateful.

As we drove along, we started talking. She said she had hitchhiked from Florida. She looked haggard, even though her skin was deeply tanned. Her face looked burned, but she had the loveliest sky-blue eyes. I could see the pain of a hard life etched onto her face. She told me she was going to the other side of Dallas, about an hour from where we were.

I had intended to take her a short distance and let her out where I thought it was safe. But again, I heard that voice. I believe the Holy Spirit said, "No, take her wherever she needs to go." I was so tired, but I had to do it.

On the way, I told her a little about the ministry, how we wanted to help women make changes in their lives. She began to relax as we drove. Suddenly, I recalled that she had been hitchhiking at almost the exact place on the road where I had picked up a woman and a baby a while back. "Are you an angel?" I asked.

She let out a startled laugh. "No, not hardly!"

I shared with her the story that had taken place eight years earlier when I had encountered an angel. The Care Ministry was in its infancy when I gave a woman and her baby a ride to her apartment. When I stopped to let them out, the most amazing thing happened. The woman and the baby had disappeared before my eyes!

For a moment I thought that this young lady would also evaporate into thin air after giving me some kind of message. Instead, she remained very human and replied, "That's nice, but I'm no angel."

As the van crept along I listened to her story. She had left Dallas because of a bad situation and had run away to Florida to start a new life. Apparently, the person she had fled from had tracked her down and demanded that she come back. She felt she had no choice but to return to a life that she feared and hated. My heart grieved for her. I knew how it felt to be a victim with no hope for the future. I began to share with her about the burden God had placed on my heart for hurting women.

I dug some money from my purse and handed it to her. "This should help you out a little," I said. She looked curiously at me as if she couldn't understand why a stranger would be willing to help her. All along that stretch of highway I silently prayed, asking the Lord to give me the opportunity to pray with her. When I finally pulled into the parking lot of the apartment building I grabbed her hand and began to pray. As I prayed I began to cry uncontrollably.

"Please don't cry for me," she begged.

Tears streamed down my cheeks. I told her, "God loves you so much!"

I saw a brokenness in her for the first time, and her face softened, becoming almost like a child's. Her eyes brimmed with tears. For a moment time seemed to stand still as we stared into each other's eyes. Perhaps she really was an angel. Who knows? And perhaps she was thinking the same thing about me.

Chapter Twenty-Three

Let Me Entertain You

She stepped into the crowded, smoke-filled room wearing almost nothing. Men surrounded the tables, drinking scotch on the rocks while waiting to be entertained by their private dancer. But she didn't mind. This particular night the dollars placed in her tiny G-string would be enough to pay for rent, groceries, clothes, and shoes for her children, and a little something for herself.

For months I had prayed to get my evangelistic feet in the door of the multimillion-dollar sex industry. Although food had been the basic type of help provided through The Care Ministry, it wasn't enough to meet the needs of women who were caught in a growing business that offered much more than groceries. Women who exploited their bodies night after night did so for the money. Topless clubs paid well, and it was no problem getting drugs before the night's show. Once the drugs kicked in, all inhibitions seemed to lift, and then the job wasn't so bad.

Jesus said, "Go into all the world and preach the good news to all creation" (Mark 16:20). To me, "all creation" included those in the sex clubs. I had business cards imprinted with my name and number, and set up another office and a separate phone line to be used as a hotline for women trapped in the sex industry. We also established a support group under the umbrella of The Care Ministry. Women from all walks of life were able to talk about their problems. They were given a safe environment where they could talk freely about their lives, answering questions no one had dared ask them before. What drove them to become a topless dancer? Why were they living in an abusive household? What were their needs? With every question, the answers varied. But the answers all stemmed from seeds of rejection and abandonment. The money provided the means of coping with a life of turmoil and despair. Nowhere else in the city could a woman bring home as much money in one day as these women made in one night.

The Bible says that the love of money is the root of all evil. The sex industry is a stark example of a seductive empire that offers more money than the average woman (or man) could make working the same amount of hours at any other job. Many of these women have never attended college and wouldn't know where to begin to find a decent job.

Meeting topless dancers through the food ministry wasn't enough. I knew it was time to go to the topless bars, just as I had visited the prisons for years. My big break came the day Amber, a topless dancer I knew, called and asked me if I would like to attend the grand opening of the newest topless club in the city. She thought it would be a great way to meet the new managers and some of the girls who would be working that night. She told me there would be a banquet and instructed me to dress in after-five attire.

The following evening I selected a pair of black crepe pants, a silk shell, and a beautiful long-sleeved sequined black jacket. I stood in front of the mirror to do a last minute makeup check. The face that stared back at me reminded me of the years of abuse. My nose was slightly crooked from being smashed by so many fists for so many years. Maybe no one would notice.

For me, abuse came in the form of a fist in the face, but abuse comes in many varieties. To the dancers, abuse was defined as exploiting their femininity simply to live. The almighty dollar lured these women into a web of seduction at the expense of their own dignity. The dollars came especially easy for the girls who performed private table dances. A girl I had met through the ministry's food distribution told me she had once made five hundred dollars in one night. I had to see what the great attraction was for the money to be so good.

Bright neon lights lit up the night sky, and I followed the blinking arrows pointing to the parking lot. I drove my car past rows of pickup trucks and nice cars until I found a vacant place. I scurried into the bar, hoping I wasn't running too late. Amber spotted me. She zigzagged her way through the crowd until we were face-to-face. The smoke and loud music made it almost impossible to carry on a conversation. We found a table and sat down. Amber grabbed my hand. "I'm really glad you came," she announced in a loud whisper. "And I'm glad you didn't see my dance."

"It's OK, really," I assured her.

And I meant it. I felt privileged to be Amber's friend as well as her special guest. I really don't know what I had expected. I wasn't there to play judge and condemn her or the other dancers.

I scanned the crowd. The room was packed with men of all ages, still in their suits and ties after a day at work. They could always say they got caught in traffic or were held up at work closing a business deal. Their wives would never know. Besides, their marriages weren't that great anyway, they'd say. As long as the bills were paid and the wife had extra spending money for the beauty parlor and lunch at the country club with friends, all was well.

Suddenly, I realized the perilous future I faced as a single woman. How on earth could I build a decent relationship with a man when the world offered this type of "gentlemen's entertainment"? How could any decent woman ever hope to get a man, much less keep him? Everywhere I looked I saw beautiful women dancing, waiting tables, standing brazenly along the walls, smiling at the passing men. Talk about a meat market!

For the first time, I understood what the game was all about. Gentlemen's entertainment is all about flesh and lust. The meaning behind the old song "Let Me Entertain You" suddenly came to light. I remembered the times when my ex-husband wanted me to seduce him by dancing for him. Now I knew where he had discovered all those things that he wanted and expected from me. I felt foolish and embarrassed for the times I tried to do a little dance, giggling like a schoolgirl, and yet wanting to be a seductive vixen waiting for the kill. Seduction was the name of the game.

I snapped back to reality as an attractive man at our table leaned over in my direction. "Do you do table dances?" He seemed a little embarrassed about his approach and smiled when I said, "Not on your life!" Amber seized the golden moment and introduced me to him and the others at the table. "This is Jackie Holland, and she is our chaplain," she said, smiling.

The man who asked me for a private dance was about ready to crawl under the table. His face turned beet red. "I am so sorry, Miss Holland. I had no idea who you were."

I flashed a smile in his direction. "It's no problem," I assured him. "I am in no way here to ruin your evening."

As it turned out he and I had a wonderful discussion about his family, his church, and his marital problems. He was not a bad man, by any means. He represented the majority of the men there who had problems and were searching for a quick, temporary fix for their inner conflicts, something to bandage the wounds of life.

He was no doubt representative of most of the men at that club. The dim lights and the seductive bodies pulsing to the beat of the music were an open invitation to taste forbidden fruit. Once the cover charge was paid, each man intended to forget all his worries and drink in as much flesh as possible. Thank God I was on divine assignment!

Looking into his eyes, I began to see clearly what was happening. God began to show me hurts and wounds on the faces of the men and women there. My heart was so sad; it would have been easy to break into tears. *God, how can I meet other people with this loud music and these topless dancers entertaining men all around me?* I thought. *How can You compete with the world?*

I excused myself from the table and disappeared into the crowd. I found a place to sit in the back of the room out of the range of roving eyes. I sat drinking my soda as I watched a couple of dancers. It was easy to see how one could get caught up in the craze of the moment. Who wouldn't want to be the center of attention if you had been rejected, abandoned, or abused your whole life? The dollar bills placed inside the edge of the tiny G-strings were a perverted validation of one's womanhood. I could see how a woman could become hardened to the crudeness, the eager hands, and the lust-filled eyes of the men. Having men want you and look at you as if they would die or kill for you at that moment surely fills a need for these love-starved and abused women. Anyone could see that.

It wouldn't be hard at all to rationalize this kind of work. Behind the so-called glamour and mystique, it's simply a job. These women work very hard. Five-inch heels make your legs look great, but think about wearing them for hours, night after night. Every man means dollars to those women, and for the most part, the men have no qualms about paying for a few minutes of thrills.

The money was good, no doubt about it. Some of the girls I talked to told me they were putting themselves through school. These were street-smart women who knew they could pull in more money in one night than they would make in a full week of flipping hamburgers or checking out groceries. That's the way everyone rationalized the clubs.

Sure, they all planned on quitting, on not getting hooked or trapped into the lifestyle. However, most women find that they can't quit because the money is so good—and because they get all the perks they need from men. On the other hand, the customers appear to be caught in the same perilous web as the women. They get a boost for their male ego, a momentary rush of pure sexual pleasure, before driving home to their wives and children. None of them think they'll get hooked on a sex-and-porn lifestyle that could control their every waking moment, all in the name of entertainment.

I met up with Amber again after her last dance, and she introduced me to Jack, the club manager, and Lucille, the housemother, as well as a few other girls. When I shared with Jack and Lucille how I wanted to be available to the girls for spiritual support, Jack said, "Sounds great. Lots of the girls here are in abusive homes and have some major drug and alcohol problems." They thanked me for coming, gladly took my business card, and gave me permission to hang posters in the dressing rooms.

David Ford, of David Ford and Associates, a local advertising agency, designed a striking poster to hang in all the dressing rooms (or maybe I should call them "undressing" rooms). The shocking pink silhouette of a shapely woman against a black background looked sleek and inviting. In boldfaced letters it read: "Give some thought to these body parts. A listening ear. A shoulder to cry on. An arm to lead. A helping hand." At the bottom of the poster we wrote the following: "Expose yourself to a new way of life. We'll show you how. Call 817-540-LADY."

I thanked Amber for the invitation. I had never once questioned whether I would visit the strip joint. For some time, it had been on my heart to infiltrate the gentlemen's clubs in our city with the love of Jesus Christ. I couldn't think of a better way to get my foot in the door than as God's representative. I proudly wore the title of chaplain.

As followers of Jesus Christ, we need to awaken out of our sleep and realize that we are the very ones who can make a difference. Everywhere I speak I tell Christians to get off their little soapboxes and start loving people. This is a mandate not only for people who are in full-time ministry but for all Christians.

If you are not called to go into dark places, send someone who is. Cover them with prayer for divine protection. You are never going to change lives by merely sitting around watching Christian television or enjoying Christian fellowship.

Jesus is coming back. Prepare the way for Him. Go and tell; go and be the light; go and help. Ask God to give resources and divine guidance to Christians. People are starving for true love, joy, and peace. They want to see realness in Christians.

Exposed Heart

When I left the club that night I had mixed feelings, of course. I had no desire to put down the clubs, but I had a real desire to tear down the walls—the walls separating light from darkness. In Matthew 7:5, Jesus said, "First take the plank out of your own eye, and then you will see clearly to remove the speck from your brother's eye." Condemnation will never bring people to Jesus. Love is the key, the only key. And God is love.

I gathered up my purse and was digging for my car keys when the man who had asked me to table dance stopped me before I walked out the door. "Would you remember to pray for my marriage?" he asked.

"Yes, of course," I answered.

I gave him my card and told him to call if he ever needed to. He said, "Thank you for caring about these girls. They really are hurting, aren't they?"

"Yes," I answered. "And will you remember to pray for me?"

He smiled and nodded.

As I walked out, no one seemed to notice. All eyes were on the girls who were moving to the beat of a different drummer.

Chapter Twenty-Four

Season of Miracles

Over a thousand people packed a Kansas City conference room waiting to hear what God would say through His servant. The prophet looked across the sea of people and asked in a heavy Indian accent, "Is someone here from Clarksville, Texas?" I raised my hand. He motioned for me to join him on the stage. I made my way past throngs of people until I came face-to-face with this messenger of God.

In the summer of 1995 a series of miracles began. I have had men and women of God speak into my life at different times, encouraging me in the work I was doing. One such word came to me when I was attending a conference in Kansas City. I was familiar with a few of the speakers, including Jack Deere, a teacher of the Word that I had grown to respect, and Mahesh Chavda, a well-known prophet, originally from India, who frequently ministers at conferences. Something had compelled me to attend this particular event.

We weren't wearing nametags, and I felt a little lost among the sea of unfamiliar faces. I listened with intensity to the men of God who shared. When Chavda began to speak to the crowd, I never expected to be called out. "Is there a Clarksville, Texas?" he asked in his thick Indian accent. This man probably didn't have a clue that Clarksville even existed. "Is someone here from Clarksville?"

I turned my head from side to side, not sure if he was talking about me. No one lifted a finger. I raised my hand. "Come up here," he instructed. I made my way up to the stage. I was shaking from head to toe.

"I see something happening in Texas," he said. "In fact, I see fire surrounding Dallas-Fort Worth. There is going to be revival coming from there. This word is a token from God."

I was born in the small northeast Texas town of Clarksville and there is no way this man could have known that the work God had called me to do was based in the Dallas-Fort Worth Metroplex. It was as if God was telling me through this prophet, *I have a purpose for your life*. I have since remembered this word during those times when I've grown weak and tired. "Wait a minute," I tell myself. "I am part of the revival coming to my city!"

More and more words began to come to me through dreams and visions. Sometimes God's voice would become almost audible. In 1997 I attended a conference in Pensacola, Florida, at the Brownsville Assembly of God, where revival had broken out and spread to the city. Thousands of people had come to the Lord, and signs and wonders were being demonstrated in the church services. I was deeply moved by the speaker's message on reconciliation among races and nationalities of people.

I didn't need to leave my hometown to minister to different cultures. Within The Care Ministry people of various ethnic backgrounds gathered under one roof: Hispanics, African Americans, Anglos, all having the same need for food, clothing, and the love of God demonstrated in a practical way.

During the Pensacola meeting one of the ministers prayed that I would receive the ministry of reconciliation of the races. Evangelist Steve Hill prayed for me and said, "Now, go and do the work of an evangelist."

After I returned home, at the weekly staff meeting one of the pastors asked me how I enjoyed the Brownsville meeting. I replied, "I am so excited—I think I could do a tent revival!" We all laughed.

I was at the post office checking my mailbox a few days after my trip and discovered a letter that caused my heart to skip a beat. It was an invitation to be a part of a large tent revival at the ballpark in Arlington, Texas, where the Texas Rangers play their home games. I had to pinch myself to make sure I wasn't dreaming!

I immediately contacted the evangelist in charge of the revival and told her I'd be there. "I sent this invitation out to over a hundred area pastors, and did you know that you are the only one who responded?" she said.

The tent revival marked the beginning of an annual summer event conducted by Sharon Bolan of Fullness of Glory Ministries.

We filled the large tent with racks of clothing and bags of food. I'm sure we looked like an awkward sight, stuffing people like sardines in a large tent in the middle of August, but I'm convinced that God likes tents...and trash bins.

Exposed Heart

Hearing God continued to be a part of my very existence. Sometimes it was easy to follow His leading, and sometimes it was difficult—like the time a few years prior God told me to give away a prized possession. I wrestled with Him as I clutched the emerald ring in the palm of my hand. It was my guarantee for a face lift and a much-needed nose job. The ring was appraised at thirteen thousand dollars, just enough to cover the cost of the plastic surgery.

My nose had been a constant source of irritation since the last time my ex-husband had broken it. Breathing was difficult, especially at night when I was lying down. I had forgotten what it was like to breathe normally, and I hated the way it bent to the right after being smashed one too many times.

As the wounds in my heart were healing, I wanted more and more to have a new nose, one that didn't remind me of my history of abuse every time I looked in the mirror. I had no significant savings. The ring would pay for the cosmetic surgery I longed to have. Again, I heard the Lord say, *Are you willing to lose everything for My sake?* It was a question I dreaded hearing. "Yes, Lord," I answered. I stared at the ring, fidgeting with it, turning it around and around, admiring the gorgeous emerald stone that held the promise of a new nose and a few less wrinkles.

The offering bucket was only a few feet away. I had to let go of my last bit of earthly security. No one told me to give it away. This was a mandate from God, although I couldn't understand His reasons at the time. Obediently, I dropped the ring in the offering bucket. My stomach did several somersaults, and I almost chased the bucket down to rescue the precious jewel. It was all I could do to let it go. I could barely sleep that night, second-guessing whether or not I had heard God correctly. But the next morning the Lord gave me a total peace that I had done the right thing.

Several weeks passed. One day my friend, Jayne Lybrand, called to tell me about a segment on the TV show *20/20* about plastic surgeons who perform free reconstructive surgery for women who had been battered. I jotted down the phone number of Dr. Jim Gilmore, a plastic surgeon in Dallas who performed such surgery. On my initial visit, I was approved for cosmetic surgery to repair my crooked nose. I couldn't believe it! God had truly rewarded my act of obedience. I had given away my ring, and God in return blessed me with the nose job I had wanted so badly. I couldn't manage to talk the Dr. Gilmore into including a face lift with the nose job. Oh well, the Lord will provide if He thinks I need one.

As the workload at The Care Ministry increased, God opened doors for community service workers to get credit for helping us sort and distribute food. Teenagers with traffic tickets and other small offenses were able to work in The Care Ministry to meet their community service requirements. Not only did they get credit for the time served, but also they heard about God's love for them and witnessed the miracle of changed lives as people came for food week after week. Also, volunteers from our church continued to multiply. God had indeed worked a miracle from a trash bin!

As crowds of people came to Happy Hour each week, the burden in my heart kept growing for the Pine Hollow apartment complex behind our church where the food was first distributed. I sensed that God wanted to open a bigger door. I met with the owner and asked him if an apartment was available for me to use to help meet the needs of the tenants. He gave me an apartment rent-free! I considered this no small miracle.

Maintenance workers replaced the damaged carpet and put a fresh coat of paint on the walls. A local furniture store donated a cherry wood dinette set, a genuine leather living room ensemble to make the apartment warm and cozy, and some beautiful pictures, one of a lighthouse on a windswept shore. I served warm cookies and beverages to those who came to our open house.

People poked their heads in and commented on how beautiful the place was. In the midst of a depressed apartment complex, here was this beacon of light—a warm, beautiful, love-filled place the tenants could call their own. I wanted it to be *theirs*. It became known as Hospitality House, where young and old alike could be tutored and where people could gather to pray or simply share their hearts and needs. It was just like God to open a door of ministry in the apartments where I had first taken the bunches of grapes and bananas twelve years earlier.

While my heart was planted at The Care Ministry, more and more opportunities arose for me to go other places to share what God had done in my life. In January of 1999 I received an invitation to attend a leadership conference in Maui, Hawaii. I was tired and in need of a retreat, so I took some vacation time and invited my friend Laquetta Dinsmore to join me. The vast blue ocean and beautiful coastline was a refreshing break from the Texas scenery. I hoped to get some sun and quality nap time in such a lovely place.

At the seminar I sat next to the pastor of the Jesus Is Alive Church in Maui. He and his wife asked if I would share my testimony at one of their services. Without hesitating I said, "Yes!"

I sensed that God wanted to do something special; I just didn't know what. During the service, as I shared the story of how God took all my failures and made something beautiful out of my life, I found myself kneeling and singing the same song Sister Saxton had sung at that revival service when I was a little girl:

"I'd like to kneel down and talk it all over with Him.

I'd like to say, Lord, You loved me when the path was so dim.

But I cannot repay Him till I meet Him in the city above,

But I'd like to talk it over and thank Him for His wonderful love."

I could feel the presence of the Holy Spirit rest on the entire congregation. "Do you want to start a food ministry?" I asked, my eyes full of tears. "Go to your pantry and take something out and give it away. Do you want to start a clothing ministry? Go to your closet and find something to give away," I pleaded. "A ministry doesn't have to start in a trash bin; it can start in your home. Give away what you have."

Silence engulfed the sanctuary as the pastor approached the microphone. "I feel like God is telling some of you to start a food ministry here in our church," he said. Several people stepped forward. Tears rolled down my cheeks, and my heart pounded with excitement. As people committed themselves to give away their time and energy to begin a food ministry in their church, a miracle of birth was happening before my eyes.

The following summer I was privileged to be part of a ministry team from Restoration Church sent to Zambia, Africa. Again, I was able to witness firsthand the power of God in the hearts of people who are seeking Him. Looking into the faces of those people was no different from looking into the hungry eyes of people who came to The Care Ministry for food week after week.

The Bible says, "Man does not live on bread alone but on every word that comes from the mouth of God" (Deuteronomy 8:3). The people in Africa were not coming to us simply to receive food and clothing; they were also coming to hear a message from God and to see His power manifested through His servants. The people of Zambia were accustomed to miracles. Many had visited witch doctors and believed in the supernatural. To be able to tell these people about Jesus and how we can have access to His miraculous healing and delivering power was awesome!

One lady who was filled with demonic spirits was set free during one of our prayer times. It took several strong men to hold her down until the demons fled from the power in the name of Jesus. Afterwards, a peace settled on this woman, and she was free!

Performing miracles isn't a hocus-pocus act we can call forth whenever we please. Miracles are about hearing what the heavenly Father wants us to do. When it is *His* will, we can move mountains. We can heal the sick. We can cast out demons. We can even raise the dead!

I returned home from my trip, eagerly anticipating what God was going to do in my own heart and city. I keep my pictures from Africa and my other trips to remind me of the faces of the people I meet. Everywhere I go, people are the same. I see the sad eyes of children, eyes that hold many secrets. I see the hopelessness and despair poverty can bring. I see emptiness in the faces of women and men who long to be loved.

Each day marks a new journey toward the hope of restoring people who are hungry and thirsty for more than food alone. "If anyone is thirsty, let him come to Me and drink. Whoever believes in Me, as the Scripture has said, streams of living water will flow from within him," Jesus said in John 7:37-38.

We live in a world where people are discarded because of poverty, prejudice, and addictions, but God sees the value in each person. He takes all their pain and mistakes and creates something beautiful. I know. He did this for me.

Chapter Twenty-Five

Winds of Change

The wind of the Spirit began blowing in a most unusual way in the summer of 1998. As The Care Ministry continued to flourish and expand—with the help of God's people working feverishly and faithfully day in and day out—I was free to follow the leading of the Holy Spirit beyond my city and church. And then, a most unexpected door opened: I was invited to minister on Bourbon Street in New Orleans. By no small coincidence, the dates of the trip included Mother's Day. I braced myself for what God was going to birth in me.

It was a balmy Saturday night when the plane touched down in New Orleans. The trip seemed to pull together at the last minute. I invited Susan, The Care Ministry coordinator, to accompany me on what proved to be an amazing journey.

It was the first time I had set foot in New Orleans, and my first impression was that it resembled a European city. Other people had prepared me for what they perceived New Orleans to be: a hot, dirty, poor, crime-infested place. If you've seen the movie *A Streetcar Named Desire,* you've seen New Orleans. Tennessee Williams made his home in the French Quarter, and he truly captured the flavor and romance of the city in the play that the movie was based on.

I had heard a lot about the French Quarter, the Cafe du Monde, Jackson Square and all the other tourist attractions. The tourist areas didn't interest me much, but I would have loved to eat at some of the fabulous restaurants I'd heard about. But as it turned out, we hardly had time to wash down a greasy hamburger with a soda.

Several months earlier I had met minister and blues guitarist Landon Spradlin while he was on business in Dallas. Landon was the outreach pastor for Cafe Joel, a Christian coffeehouse located right in the heart of the French Quarter on Bourbon Street. The coffeehouse was located in one of those charming, three-story French colonial buildings laced with wrought iron that gives the French Quarter its distinctive ambiance.

Cafe Joel, an outreach of Victory Fellowship of Metairie, Louisiana, was on the second floor, sandwiched between a private residence on the top floor and a street-level club called The Gay Paree, which featured live orgies every night and photos of the floorshow on a marquee outside. We called it The Orgy for short. Two doors down is a place called Big Daddies: Topless and Bottomless. It has a very distinctive sign: a pair of slender mannequin legs in high heels swinging out rhythmically above your head. If I momentarily got lost, I could always find my way back by that sign!

Landon has a heart for ministering to street people. He came to know many of the managers, dancers, bouncers, bartenders and performers that work in the French Quarter and wanted to start an outreach to minister to exotic dancers, but he knew that a man could not head up that effort. He needed a mature Christian woman to direct, implement and oversee such a ministry.

One day while he was praying, he sensed that the Lord was telling him to call me. We both shared the desire to minister to exotic dancers, and immediately we began making arrangements for me to join him in starting Exotic Dancers Outreach, which was very much like the ministry I had to dancers in the topless clubs in Dallas.

Landon picked us up at the New Orleans airport and suggested that we walk the French Quarter that night to get a feel for the place. We drove over an enormous bridge that spans the Mississippi, and before I knew it we were walking up Bourbon Street. Suddenly, I heard the Lord say, "I have given you an open door that no man can shut."

The area was teeming with people, strolling up and down one of the most famous streets in the world, ready to forget their worries by giving themselves over to a night that promised to fulfill all of their fantasies. Many were bleary-eyed and staggering as they wandered from club to club. The doors to the nightclubs and strip joints were wide open, with jazz and blues music blaring in the background. People spilled out from the clubs looking for the next thrill. As I stood on the sidewalk I could peer between people's shoulders to see scantily clad women gyrating in the spotlight before a rapt crowd.

Exposed Heart

People from all over the world come to visit New Orleans. Sharply dressed doctors, businessmen, young couples with children in strollers, older couples, college students, runaways, young singles, bikers, musicians, visitors from Europe and other foreign areas were all there to experience what Bourbon Street promised—fun and pleasure.

One large group of young people who congregate on Bourbon Street is the Goths. They dress in black, wear black lipstick, paint their nails black, do wild things with their hair and sport multiple body piercings. Many of these kids are homeless and sleep on the river levee behind the Cafe du Monde. No doubt some have been attracted to New Orleans in part by Anne Rice's "Vampire" book series, which features an aboveground cemetery in the city. Scores of fortunetellers and artists ply their trades on Jackson Square in front of St. Louis Cathedral, and a famous voodoo shop, Marie Leveau's, sells voodoo paraphernalia. For whatever reason, the Goths make Bourbon Street their home.

After walking the French Quarter we went up to Cafe Joel. We met Lance, a wonderful brother in the Lord from Jamaica. He is Landon's right-hand man, a quiet, fearless, godly man who speaks with the lilting grace of his homeland. Then we met Roxanne, a former exotic dancer, and her boyfriend, Michael. The first time I saw Roxanne, she was sitting on the second-story balcony of Cafe Joel gazing at the passing crowds. I looked up and waved at her, and she pretended not to notice me. She had just gotten out of jail after her arrest for public drunkenness.

Roxanne's parents were in their forties with grown children when she was born. She was raised in Biloxi, Mississippi, mostly by her oldest brother and his wife. As a child she was sexually abused by an uncle, but when she told her family, many of her relatives refused to believe her and rejected her as a result. Her family fell apart over this incident, and Roxanne was made the scapegoat. Starting at the age of ten, she ran away many times to escape the abuse. That got her into trouble with the police, but the police never dealt with the real problem, the sexual abuse by her uncle.

Roxanne suffered from a serious problem with rejection. Some people who have a spirit of rejection retreat inside themselves and let people stomp all over them; others become "in-your-face" combative. Roxanne fell into the latter category. When anyone hurt her, she would strike back by yelling and pitching a fit. She's not one to suffer abuse silently, and when she mixes alcohol with her temperament, she gets a ticket straight to jail.

Roxanne came downstairs with Michael, who had just returned from North Carolina and spent his last dime bailing her out of jail. Michael is a tall, lanky man whose dirty blonde hair frames the haunting eyes that are set into his deeply lined face. Hardship, worry and sadness made him look much older than he really was. Michael and Roxanne talked a little about how they were trying to pull a few dollars together for a room for the night; Landon gave them some money before we went upstairs.

After introducing us to everyone at Cafe Joel, Landon escorted us around the French Quarter and showed us all the exotic dance clubs—eighteen in the Quarter alone. It was getting late, and we had to get up early to go to church. I knew before we left Dallas that this was going to be a special trip. As I laid my head down on the pillow that night and looked up into the darkness, Susan and I talked across the room and wondered what God had planned for us.

Landon picked us up at the hotel the next morning and took us to Metairie, a suburb of New Orleans where Victory Fellowship is located. The pastors, Frank and Paris Bailey, welcomed us with open arms. The Holy Spirit surged like a river through the church. Because it was Mother's Day, Pastor Frank spoke on the mother heart of God. My ears perked up, since The Care Ministry's motto is "The Father's Heart With a Mother's Touch." What he said touched me so deeply that I wept through the entire service. God is the Father, he said, but He is also the Mother. Jesus wept over Jerusalem, saying, "O Jerusalem, Jerusalem...how often I have longed to gather your children together as a hen gathers her chicks under her wings" (Luke 13:34). The father rooster is bold and defends his brood with the spurs on his legs. When the mother hen senses danger, she backs up, splays her wings, gathers her babies beneath her wings and juts out her breast. She lets her enemies know that they are going to have to go through her to get her babies. God is like that.

It became a nightly ritual to go out with Landon and minister on the streets. First we would pray from nine to ten o'clock and then hit the streets until around midnight. I met with many people in the clubs and was graciously received everywhere I went. At one point one of the bouncers chased after me as I walked down the street, shouting "Miss Holland, Miss Holland, I need more of your business cards. I gave all the rest away!"

Everywhere I went I told the people who worked in the clubs about a banquet Landon and I were planning, sponsored by Cafe Joel. One particular club employed female impersonators to dance and to entertain the crowds. I entered the club somewhat leery about how I would respond to a man dressed up like a woman. A dancer approached me, and we began to talk. I was stunned at how much this man looked like a woman. He wore a flamboyant outfit and blonde wig, his nails were painted, and he had a gorgeous figure. I would have never known this person was a man.

"You're so beautiful," he said.

I looked into his made-up eyes and saw the pain buried beneath the false eyelashes. "Well, you're beautiful too. I hope you can come to the banquet," I said.

"I don't know if you want me to come," he muttered.

"Why wouldn't I want you to come?" I asked.

The dancer replied hesitantly, "Well, I'm not really a woman."

"Well, do you see yourself as a man...or a woman?" I asked gently.

The dancer responded, "I'm not sure."

"You come. We would love to have you," I assured him.

Thursday morning we woke up bright and early to meet with Landon and get the final details worked out for the banquet. I was both nervous and excited. Although we had been in New Orleans only six days, it had seemed like a month. We hadn't read a paper, watched TV, or listened to the radio the whole time. All I could think about was the banquet.

One of Landon's friends, Darrel, is the manager of a men's homeless shelter in an old white building on the edge of the Quarter. He and some other men volunteered to prepare the banquet meal. We quickly arrived to set up and dress the tables with tablecloths and flowers. We were so busy making our preparations that the time sped by, and before we knew it our guests were arriving.

Exposed Heart

About fifteen women from Victory Fellowship and ten men and women dancers as well as club employees came to the banquet. Roxanne showed up in her very best clothes. She was wearing a pretty black dress, lipstick and mascara. We served non-alcoholic drinks and an array of finger foods. I shared my testimony and Landon sang "He Is There." We prayed for people's needs. And God was faithful to bless each and every person who came. These were truly the people God had been speaking to me about; He clearly wants me—and all of us—to reach out to the outcast and lonely.

When God is involved, there are no chance encounters—only divine appointments. One night, a man pulled his young wife up the stairs to Cafe Joel, thinking it was The Orgy. I talked with the couple at the door and invited them in, but they backed out of the doorway when they found out where they were. I said a prayer for them as they turned on their heels and fled down the stairs, out onto the street and into the reveling crowds.

I wasn't surprised to run into them again the next day. I recognized them immediately and said, "Hi. It's nice to see you again!" The couple blurted out a stunned hello and took off in embarrassment. I turned to Susan and said, "Divine appointments—you can run...but you cannot hide!"

Late one morning we dressed and took a taxi to the French Quarter for lunch. We ate lunch in a little Cajun restaurant right across from St. Louis Cathedral. It was a small, informal place, with café-style tables dressed in white tablecloths that dotted the room and spilled out on to the sidewalk. Our table was in front of one of the many pairs of tall doors that doubled as windows. The breeze was soft and balmy. People strolled by as we leisurely ate our gumbo and etouffee.

As we were sitting there, a thought suddenly struck me—and my eyes brimmed over with tears. Susan looked at me with inquiring eyes. "I just realized something. God birthed The Care Ministry on Father's Day. Now He has birthed a women's outreach in New Orleans on Mother's Day!" I cried.

I knew in my heart that this was the first of many such outreaches that would be birthed throughout the country.

Epilogue

After all of my marriages and my experiences with men—especially abusive men—some might think that I have no desire to ever share my life with a man again. Others may wonder how I've learned to live as a single woman after being married for so long and so many times.

Several years ago I was talking to the Lord about this very subject. I wanted to know His will, and I sensed Him say this to me: "You don't need a man. You need many men—men who have a heart for Me, who believe in what you're doing and will support the work in various ways." The Lord impressed on me that I am not to try to make *anything* happen, whether it be with regard to marriage or ministry. I am to trust Him and be faithful, remaining open to His leading, should he provide an opportunity for marriage or a different ministry.

The Bible says that "He who finds a find a wife finds a good thing and obtains favor from the Lord." Proverb 18:22 I might be "found" in the future but I'm certainly not looking for a husband or running ads proclaiming my singleness or trying to be at the right place at the right time to meet the ever-elusive Mr. Right. I have a few truly good friends—men and women—that I occasionally go to dinner or to a movie. They respect the call of God on my life. So far, the Lord has not put that "You're-the-one-for-me" feeling in my heart for any of the men I know. I am single and content with that.

As for my children, despite everything they've endured with me—the divorces, fights, abuse, financial struggles, the time I wasn't able to give them—they have always been accepting and supportive of my ministry. I am so thankful for and proud of them.

My daughter, Charlsey is happily married. She is a wonderful mother, wife and daughter. She has always respected and honored me. She loves to make things like hooked rugs, needlepoint and other craft items for me. She is a beautiful person, inside and out, and although we missed some years together, when we get together now we make every minute count and have so much fun together. Her son, Isaiah, loves the Word and says he is going to be a missionary when he grows up.

My son Howard, with his dark, dimpled good looks, struggled with depression following his father's departure and Mikey's death. His first marriage also failed, and he has battled drugs and alcohol. He reminds me a lot of myself when I was younger. I have been on my knees for years interceding for him; God told me a long time ago that when He looks at Howard He sees a mighty man of valor. I know he loves the Lord and that his life is changing every day.

I am hoping that in God's timing my relationship with my two precious stepchildren will be restored. I love them; they are such beautiful children! I have received photos of their children over the years. They love the Lord, and I am looking for Him to do great things in their lives.

What can I say about my mother except that she is wonderful! She is always there for me. She attends the same church I do and when I am in town we always spend Sunday afternoon together. She grows the most beautiful flowers and bakes the most luscious desserts. More and more I treasure our time together. God and family are her life; she loves people, but she adores her children. A lovely Muslim woman gave her a precious little dog shortly after my father died. Mother named her Sugar, and they are now inseparable.

I am happy to say my sisters and brother are all sincere and dedicated Christians. We don't get to spend a lot of time with each other, but if one little crisis comes up everyone comes together. My father believed the scripture, "Believe in the Lord Jesus Christ, and you will be saved—you and your household" (Acts 16:31). He taught us to believe that too, and we have confidence that all of our children will eventually serve the Lord.

APPENDIX

DEPRESSION SYMPTOMS AND RESOURCES

I wish I had known as much about depression before my son committed suicide as I do now. While I certainly believe the Lord can and does heal all diseases and disorders, He also works through the medical and mental health communities—as well as medications—to help suffering people. Much of the suffering that stems from depression is unnecessary, but those afflicted with the disorder need help—and the support of friends and family who will assist them in getting the kind of help they need. I pray that the following information will enable you to recognize depression in yourself or those around you and to seek out the resources that offer relief from this often psychologically and emotionally debilitating condition.

Each year, about 19 million Americans suffer from depression—and countless people around them are affected as well. Depression interferes with a person's ability to function normally and can lead to the destruction of family life, or worse, to suicide.

Many depressed people don't seek help, often because they're unaware that it's a treatable illness. The more you learn about the symptoms and treatments of depression, the more likely it is that you will be able to help a depressed person—and possibly save his or her life.

Depression is:

- an illness that affects the body, mind and spirit.
- a disorder that often alters a person's sleep routine, appetite, self-esteem, behavior and thought processes.
- treatable through counseling, sometimes in combination with antidepressant medications.

Depression is not:

- the normal sadness a person may feel every now and then.
- a sign of personal weakness.
- a disorder that can be "cured" through determination or wishful thinking.

SYMPTOMS OF DEPRESSION

- Persistent sad, anxious or "empty" mood
- Feelings of hopelessness or pessimism
- Feelings of guilt, worthlessness and helplessness
- Loss of interest or pleasure in hobbies and activities that were once enjoyed, including sex

- Fatigue, decrease in energy, a feeling of being "slowed down"
- Difficulty concentrating, remembering or making decisions
- Insomnia, early-morning awakening or oversleeping
- Appetite loss and weight loss, or overeating and weight gain
- Thoughts of death or suicide; suicide attempts
- Restlessness, irritability
- Persistent physical symptoms that do not respond to treatment, such as headaches, digestive disorders and chronic pain

IF YOU ARE DEPRESSED...

- Set realistic goals and assume a reasonable amount of responsibility.
- Break large tasks into small ones, set priorities and do what you can as you can.
- Try to be with other people and to confide in someone; it is usually better than being alone and secretive.
- Participate in activities that may make you feel better.
- Mild exercise, going to a movie, a ballgame or participating in religious, social or other activities may help.
- Expect your mood to improve gradually, not immediately. Feeling better takes time.
- Postpone important decisions until the depression has

lifted; discuss them with others who know you well and have a more objective view of your situation.
- Don't expect an immediate "cure"—but you can expect to feel a little better day by day.
- Practice positive thinking.
- Let your family and friends help you.

WHERE TO GET HELP:

National Institute of Mental Health
6001 Executive Boulevard
Bethesda, MD 20892-9663
(301) 443-4513
Depression brochures: (800) 421-4211
TTY: (301) 443-8431
E-mail: *nimhinfo@nih.gov*
Web site: *http://www.nimh.nih.gov*

National Alliance for the Mentally Ill
Colonial Place Three
2107 Wilson Blvd., Suite 300
Arlington, VA 22201-3042
(703) 524-7600; (800) 950-NAMI
Web site: *http://www.nami.org*

National Depressive and Manic Depressive Association
730 N. Franklin, Suite 501
Chicago, IL 60601
(312) 642-0049; (800) 826-3632
Web site: *http://www.ndmda.org*

National Foundation for Depressive Illness
P.O. Box 2257
New York, NY 10016
(212) 268-4260; (800) 239-1265
Web site: *http://www.depression.org*

National Mental Health Association
1021 Prince Street
Alexandria, VA 22314-2971
(703) 684-7722; (800) 969-6642
TTY: (800) 433-5959
Web site: *http://www.nmha.org*

Christian Resources:

Christian Therapy Program
Dr. Fred Gross
570 Glenneyre Avenue, Suite 107
Laguna Beach, CA 92651
(800) HELP-4-ME
Affiliated with New Life Treatment Centers

LifeCare Christian Therapy Centers
Fred Kendall
1210 S. Adams
 Fort Worth, TX 76104
(800) PSALMS 91

New Life Clinics
Steven Arterburn and Dr. Paul Meier
570 Glenneyre Avenue, Suite 107
Laguna Beach, CA 92651
(800) NEW-LIFE
Adolescent and adult care

Rapha Hospital Treatment
Bruce Cook
5500 Interstate North Parkway, Suite 515
Atlanta, GA 30328
(800) 383-HOPE
Adolescent & adult care

Tennessee Christian Counseling Center
Tennessee Christian Medical Center
600 Medical Park Drive, Suite 204
Madison, TN 37115
(615) 860-6500
Outpatient and group counseling
Adolescent and adult care

Information on depression adapted from materials provided by the National Institute of Mental Health.

1 This is me at 12 years old
2 Sonny and I, shortly after getting married
3 My children

1 Jeannie Turner and I at "One Way Out"
2 Ministry for Hurting Women
3 Here I am with evangelist Barry Mason
(ex Hell's Angel President)
4 In Zambia at a remote village

1 My grandaughter Alexis Hope Holland
2 My grandson Isaiah Daniel Bock
3 My mother and daughter Charlsey
4 My son Howard

1 Happy days with Mr Bill (102 years old)
2 My grandaughter Cierra Laura Holland

1 Here we are in 1946, Barbara, Marita, Don & me
2 My son Mike on his graduation day
3 Here we are again, my dad, mom, sisters and my brother Don